WINNING IN LIFE

WINNING IN LIFE

Rob Ellis

Good Life Publishing
Troy, Michigan

Good Life Publishing
P.O. Box 393
Troy, Michigan 48099

Copyright © 2009 by Robert T. Ellis

All rights reserved. This book is protected by the copyright laws of the United States of America. This book may not be copied or reprinted for commercial gain or profit. The use of short quotations and occasional page copying for personal or group study is permitted and encouraged. Permission may be granted upon request.

Unless otherwise identified, Scripture quotations are from the King James Version of the Bible.

Scripture identified by NKJV taken from the New King James Version Copyright © 1979, 1980, 1982 by Thomas Nelson, Inc. Used by permission. All rights reserved.

ISBN-13: 978-0-615-30615-5
ISBN-10: 0615306152

For Worldwide Distribution

Printed in the U.S.A.

10 9 8 7 6 5 4 3 2 1

Special Thanks

To my mother, Delores Ellis, who is responsible for instilling in me Christian values, strength and perseverance.

Dedication

To my wife, Deborah, and my two sons, Roberto and Chad.

Table of Contents

Introduction: Winning is a Process 1
Chapter 1: The "I" in Team 3
Chapter 2: Discovering Who You Are 7
Chapter 3: The Winner's Attitude 12
Chapter 4: Setting Your Goals 17
Chapter 5: Acknowledging the Team 23
Chapter 6: 3 Strategies for Winning 31
Chapter 7: 3 Keys to Activating Your Faith 46
Chapter 8: Forming Your Team 60
Chapter 9: Move into Action 79
Chapter 10: 3 Keys to Maintaining Victory 93
Chapter 11: Share Your Story 103
Chapter 12: The Greatest Investment 113

Introduction: Winning is a Process

"The faster, the better," most will say when it comes to achieving a goal. It can be very tempting to make haste toward your desired destination. Yes, timing is very important. However, it is the rushing that often leads to the half-doing that ultimately prevents most from excelling to higher heights of achievement and recognition in record time.

Winning isn't so much about speed as it is about endurance and integrity. It's not just about getting there. *How* you get there is just as—if not more—important. Your journey toward personal success won't be measured by how fast you get there so much as it will be remembered for the quality of your experience getting there, and your ability to share such experience with others.

Winning in life is a process...

And it is never completed by accident. If your intent is true and godly success, you must have a strategy: a game plan; an adequate, if not exceptional, understanding of what it will take to achieve your goals. What will be required of you? What must you require of others? How will it all unfold?

...So, what does it take to win?

The answer begins with you. You are what you believe in; you do what you know. What you practice and feed into your spirit will affect every area of your life, especially your race toward the finish line. Therefore, be careful not to allow erroneous beliefs and bad habits to travel with you on your journey toward success. Rather, equip yourself with the knowledge necessary to make good decisions and not only cross the finish line, but also feel good about yourself once you've crossed it.

In this book you will discover steps and hidden paths to achieving your visions, goals and dreams. You will come to a greater understanding of who you are and what you bring to the table. With God's help, you will accomplish great things as you learn invaluable strategies for "Winning in Life."

Chapter 1:
The "I" in Team

Everyone wants to be a success; no one wants to be a failure. Everyone wants to win in life... In this life, there are two types of winners: those who earn the finish line, and those standing at the finish line cheering on the victor, having supported him all along.

In other words, some people win because they did everything that they personally needed to do to win the race. They determined in their minds to win. They trained to endure the pains of the fight and the length of the course. They learned how to avoid pitfalls and costly mistakes—how to overcome setbacks and never give up, despite the odds. They learned how to not only size up their opponents, but also how to size up themselves. They came to know both their strengths and weaknesses, and the internal wherewithal that would eventually render them success.

The other type of winner wins by association. They are preferred to share in the experience of the victor because of what they mean to him: the teacher, the wife, the best friend, the biggest fan. Although these people did not run the same type of race, they are winners nonetheless because they exist as the motivation behind the victor out front. They serve as the inspiration that makes it all worthwhile for him.

Winning is never a solo act. Therefore, if you desire to win in this life, you must first discover which type of winner you are to be: the bow or the arrow. Then you must embrace the people that will help you fulfill your destiny. And that's the secret to winning—right here at the very beginning of this book!

If you want to win, you need to be on the right team.

Now, it's been said that there's no "I" in "team." This saying is typically used to admonish the team member that may think he's more important to the effort than the other members. Truly, the most successful team efforts rarely have room for the burden of "Big I's".

However, while there isn't an "I" in "team," there certainly is an "I" in "win." Therefore, if you desire to experience personal success—to *personally* win—you must never lose sight of the fact that ultimately such can only be measured by whether or not you personally cross the finish line. No matter how great your team, if you don't meet your personal goals, you will find yourself living a life of unfulfilled dreams.

Perhaps your goal is to be a millionaire, or maybe you just want to get your children through college. Maybe you've been commissioned to preach the Gospel or perhaps you're searching to cure AIDS. Whether your goal is to see the success of others or yourself, if you personally invest yourself toward such success—and win—it is a personal success.

We each live different lives. Each person's race is different. Truly, successes are defined in so many different ways so that no two are exactly alike. Still, all successes have this in common: the proper execution of both timing and effort toward a goal of some sort.

Therefore, the team is made of many individuals racing for a shared cause. Think of it as a marathon in which every one wins. And if you grasp this concept, not a single person on your team will ever feel under-appreciated or out of place, because each will know his value and his place. Each will have his own goals being fulfilled by the efforts of the entire team. In this way, "team" is entirely composed of "I's".

And ultimately, the Biggest "I" on your team should be our Lord and Savior Jesus Christ. For it is in Him that we live, and move, and have our being. (Acts 17:28) The Bible says that, "...we are more than conquerors through him that loved us." (Romans 8:37) Without a doubt, you need Jesus Christ on your team if you're going to win in this life, and the one to come. It is his unconditional love that triumphs over fear and doubt, leading us into the discovery of who we are and what we can be.

On the road of life, it is His word that will be the lamp unto your feet, and the light unto your path. (Psalm 119:105) Jesus is the ultimate support and resource toward victory because He not only wants you to win, but is ever-present to help you do it. Jesus said in His word, "Beloved, *I* wish above all things that you would prosper and be in health, even as your soul prospers." (3 John 1:2) It is God's personal goal to see you succeed so that His Glory would be revealed in and through your life.

So there is an "I" in "team" after all. You are that "I" and God's on your team just as you are on His. Still, this doesn't mean that God will do all the work for you. In fact, you (and the other members of your team) will do a lot of it yourself. And it probably won't be easy—certainly, easier said than done. However, it can be done. It has been done. And if you want it, I can show you how it's done…

Let us examine the art of winning: the art of self-discovery, dynamic teamwork, and personal success.

Chapter 2: Discovering Who You Are

Winning begins with a goal: a target. Without focus, there is no sight. Without cause, there is no effect. Without a goal, you cannot win. Period. And your first goal should be to discover who you are, and *whose* you are.

Who are you?

Answering this question will determine what kind of winner you can become. Remembering that there are two types of winners, similarly, there are two types of people: the one running out front, and the support cheering him on. They work together toward a common goal, toward a target—like a bow and arrow. So, to rephrase the question, which are you, a *bow* or an *arrow*?

Arrows are assertive personalities: they're always out front. They possess the attitude and courage of champions; they believe that they can do anything and people tend to depend on them to defeat the Goliath's of life. You'll rarely hear an Arrow utter the words, "I can't." Their mentality is always, "I can." And above all, they desire to succeed and will settle for nothing short of nailing the target right on the head.

Bows tend to be more passive. However, such should not be mistaken for weakness. Whereas an Arrow sometimes easily breaks under certain conditions, enduring those same conditions, a Bow will bend and flex, turning the tension of the situation into the very power needed to thrust the team forward. A Bow will always say, "You can do it" and "We can do it!" They're always there to help, and are of great necessity. Without a Bow, an Arrow will never reach its goals.

They need one another, Bows and Arrows. So again, the question, which one are you?

Typically, from a young age, you and the people around you will have some sense of who you are. In the best case scenario, your potential will be developed.

Unfortunately, life is not always the "best case scenario." More often, life is the "real case scenario." And too often, we grow up not knowing our potential, let alone having it developed. We grow up saying, "I can't," and "You can't." We get beat up by life, and develop the unregenerated mentality of someone who has stopped trying to reach his goals: the mentality of a failure. We find ourselves unable to, with any good report, answer the question, "Who am I?"

It is important to understand that you are whoever God says you are. And in God's eyes you are a child of the King and you belong to Him.

The Bible tells us that, "...he hath chosen us in him before the foundation of the world, that we should be holy and without blame before him in love: Having predestinated us unto the adoption of children by Jesus Christ to himself, according to the good pleasure of his will... we have obtained an inheritance, being predestinated according to the purpose of him who works all things after the counsel of his own will." (Ephesians 1:4-5, 11)

God has a specific plan for the life of every individual. Each of us is predestined for a tailored greatness by His design. As a child of the King, we have an inheritance that includes everything we could possibly want or need in this life and the one to come—everything!

Money: God already sees you financially prosperous. Health: God desires for you to be alive and well. Family and friends: God means for you to live in a community of people that love and care for you. Peace of mind, strength, courage, wisdom—winning in life, a child of the King!

To the extent that they are necessary for your success, all these things are yours in Him. However, you will never access them if you don't know that they are for you. And you will never know that they are for you if you don't understand who you are, and the rights and privileges afforded to you by virtue of such. God created you a Bow or Arrow uniquely designed to nail a particular target. And He's committed to providing you with everything that you need to meet the goal.

So, knowing who you are is of the utmost importance. Your success is contingent upon this discovery. In the Bible, often great men and women of God went through a trying period of self-discovery before realizing their destinies and accomplishing goals of biblical proportions. The harder the trial period, the greater the success:

Abraham had to leave the comfort zone of familiar surroundings before he would become the father of many nations. Joseph endured slavery for decades before he became one of the highest ranking officials in all of Egypt. Moses went through the desert before he met God on Mount Sinai and delivered Israel. The widow Ruth faithfully followed Naomi throughout the harvest season before marrying Boaz! Even Jesus fasted for 40 days and nights, tried by Satan himself, before launching a dynamic ministry that would save the world!

Therefore, you should also embrace the challenges sent to develop you, key investments toward the revelation of who you are, whether you're a Bow or an Arrow.

Understanding who you are and the value placed on your life comes from understanding God's investment in your life. Everything that God has for you is already set aside for you. All His promises were settled before the foundation of the world.

The Bible says, "For all the promises of God in him are yea, and in him Amen, unto the glory of God by us." (2 Corinthians 1:20) Does God want you to win? Yes. Does He want you to prosper? Yes. In every area of life? Yes and Amen!

Ask yourself, "What has God promised me?" In a word, God has promised you success. It is His plan to use you and those around you to manifest that success, according to His will. And this begins with understanding the gift and calling God's placed on your life.

What are you good at doing? What do you like to do? What do you want? Where would you like to go? What can you handle? Are you use to helping others? All of these questions point in the direction of your gift and calling. And in more than a few cases, the possibilities are only limited by your ability to visualize and step out on God's word.

Jesus said, "If you abide in me, and my words abide in you, you shall ask what you will, and it shall be done unto you." (John 15:7) There is no limit to what God can do for you and through you. Therefore, it is ultimately up to you as to whether or not you will step out on faith, "...confident of this very thing, that he which hath begun a good work in you will perform it until the day of Jesus Christ." (Philippians 1:6)

Which one are you: a Bow or an Arrow? Whatever your answer, be confident in the professing and exploration thereof. Be confident that there is a purpose for your life, and a place for you on a winning team. And as you discover the potential within, nothing will be more crucial for its cultivation than having a winner's attitude.

Chapter 3:
The Winner's Attitude

Attitude is a choice. No, we don't always have a choice as to what will happen to us. But we always have a choice as to how we will react. However the race begins, your attitude is definitely a determining factor as to how it proceeds and how it ends. Why? Because your attitude affects your behavior. It has a profound influence on the way that you perceive things and the decisions that you make based on your perceptions. What's more, your attitude not only affects you, but everyone around you as well: team members and opponents alike.

What is the winner's attitude?

To sum it up, the winner's attitude is having a positive disposition and feeling toward winning. Do you want to win? Do you tend to only want the best? Or are you orientated toward concession, settling for whatever's left over? Acquiring the winner's attitude begins with the mentality that you *must* win. No room for doubt or second guessing. Make up in your mind that failure is not an option. When you start winning, losing becomes unpalatable. It just doesn't taste good. Even if you should lose the battle, winning the war remains in sight, and in the winner's mind, it is the only acceptable outcome. And it's not arrogant to say so.

Some people actually have a problem saying, "I'm a winner." They have a problem with thinking highly of themselves—yes "highly," not to be confused with thinking "more highly than you ought." (Romans 12:3) As is too often the case, at some point they were erroneously taught that the virtue of humility is signified by a down-trodden self-image. However, nothing could be farther from the truth.

Jesus Christ, the humblest of all men, had no problem saying, "In the world you shall have tribulation: but be of good cheer; I have overcome the world." (John 16:33) To overcome the world with all its hardships is no small feat, and yet Christ had no reservations about boasting in this godly victory. Moreover, He encourages us to do the same, "You are of God, little children, and have overcome them (the world): because greater is he that is in you, than he that is in the world." (1 John 4:4)

So, if the Holy Spirit within you is great enough to take on the whole world, what is it that you can't accomplish in your personal life? And why would you ever settle for anything other than total victory in every task that you set out to do?

Attitude.

It starts in your mind. The Bible instructs us to, "...be not conformed to this world: but be ye transformed by the renewing of your mind, that ye may prove what is that good, and acceptable, and perfect, will of God."

Often a mental transformation is necessary to undo years of false teaching and all the negative conditioning that has made you comfortable with failure—or even ignorant of the fact that you're failing.

The winner's attitude never denies that failures and obstacles exists, or underestimates the magnitude of them. Rather, the winner's attitude chooses to have faith that failures and obstacles can be overcome, magnifying the power of God that is ever-present and well-able to help you accomplish the task.

It is no secret that our goals are often and usually met with obstacles. Obstacles surface to either halt, inhibit, or deter your progress. Whether you succeed or fail, whether you overcome or "under-come" is all determined by how you react to the obstacles in your life, determined by your attitude. Truly, your mind is the battlefield. If you can win in your mind, half the battle's already won. Then, the second half of the battle will be won as you face the obstacles and challenges ahead.

To acquire the winner's attitude, you must learn to confess those things that will build you up and mentally prepare you for success, "Finally, brethren, whatsoever things are true, whatsoever things are honest, whatsoever things are just, whatsoever things are pure, whatsoever things are lovely, whatsoever things are of good report; if there be any virtue, and if there be any praise, think on these things." (9 Philippians 4:8)

Change your thoughts, and you will certainly change your attitude. No matter how dark the situation, choose to see the light at the end of the tunnel—and no, it's not an oncoming train! It's the brilliance and guiding power of the Holy Spirit!

Remember you control your thoughts and what you say. Make the choice to dwell on and confess those things that are aligned with God's promises and His plan for your life, "Casting down imaginations, and every high thing that exalts itself against the knowledge of God, and bringing into captivity every thought to the obedience of Christ." (2 Corinthians 10:5)

It can be difficult at first, if you're use to thinking the wrong thing. If your attitude is typically guided by your emotions and the woes of the situation at hand, then you've got a lot of work to do. But you don't have to do it alone. God will keep you in perfect peace as long as your mind is stayed on Him. (Isaiah 26:3) You just have to trust Him.

You must trust God, beyond the sarcasm and bad reports. Trust Him in spite of the doubters, the haters, and the naysayers. Trust Him and say within yourself, "Let the words of my mouth, and the meditation of my heart, be acceptable in thy sight, O Lord, my strength." (Psalm 19:14)

This is the art of positive confession: the winner's attitude. And once you've acquired the right attitude, it is vitally important that you maintain it from start to finish.

Sometimes we are guilty of starting the race with bright spirits. But after a while, as the work becomes more tedious and energy begins to wane, we lose focus and enthusiasm—and sometimes, we even give up just before the finish line! But that's not the winner's attitude.

Winners always finish the race: they endure the fight until the very end. Don't give up! No matter what, don't give up! At all times, your attitude must be, "fight the good fight."

What's a good fight? One in which you win!

"Wherefore take unto you the whole armour of God, that you may be able to withstand in the evil day, and having done all, to stand! Stand." (Ephesians 6:14)

Chapter 4:
Setting Your Goals

Let's be honest. When it comes to goal setting, many—if not most of us—have set out to be millionaires.

But it's not about the millions. Well, maybe it is for you. However, that would be a very narrow way of defining your goals and success. After you've discovered who you are and acquired the right attitude, setting your goals is the next biggest step. And if you're not careful, it can be oh too easy to make the mistake of setting a big, elaborate goal that has nothing to do with your purpose.

Yes, you have a purpose, a godly purpose. If a million dollars is necessary or even desirable toward the fulfillment of that godly purpose, then bring on the millions! Even so, it's still not about the millions. It's about the purpose.

Whether it's money, health, or good company, everything has a purpose. It was Miles Monroe that said, "If one does not understand the purpose of a thing, abuse is inevitable." This is a true saying that is particularly relevant to goal setting. Many people set goals as if the goals are an end unto themselves. Typically, they seek the things they see others with, and go after these things "just because." Granted, we all like nice things. There's nothing wrong with having nice things. Again, however, even if you go after something nice "just because," without having a clear understanding of its purpose or how it will affect your purpose, abuse is inevitable.

God grants us various gifts and talents for the purpose of building His kingdom. 1 Peter 2:9 tells us that you are "...a chosen generation, a royal priesthood, an holy nation, a peculiar people; that you should show forth the praises of him who hath called you out of darkness into his marvelous light." Ultimately this is His will for your life: that you would show forth His Glory in the Earth.

Granted, God gets no Glory out of you being broke, busted and disgusted. Resources are necessary for the kingdom, and befitting for the children of the King. Howbeit, what you do with the resources that God gives you—and, just as important, *why* you do what you do—will determine whether or not you fulfill your purpose in Him.

Consider the parable of the talents from Matthew 25: 14-29:

> For the kingdom is like a man going on a journey, who summoned his servants and entrusted his property to them. To one he gave five talents, to another two, and to another one, each according to his ability. Then he went on his journey. The one who had received five talents went off right away and put his money to work and gained five more. In the same way, the one who had two gained two more. But the one who had received one talent went out and dug a hole in the ground and hid his master's money in it.

After a long time, the master of those servants came and settled his accounts with them. The one who had received the five talents came and brought five more, saying, "Sir, you entrusted me with five talents. See, I have gained five more." His master answered, "Well done, good and faithful servant! You have been faithful in a few things. I will put you in charge of many things. Enter into the joy of your master." (NKJV)

***

The one with the two talents also came and said, "Sir, you entrusted two talents to me. See, I have gained two more." His master answered, "Well done, good and faithful servant! You have been faithful with a few things. I will put you in charge of many things. Enter into the joy of your master."

Then the one who had received the one talent came and said, "Sir, I knew that you were a hard man, harvesting where you did not sow, and gathering where you did not scatter seed, so I was afraid, and I went and hid your talent in the ground. See, you have what is yours."

But his master answered, "Evil and lazy servant! So you knew that I harvest where I didn't sow and gather where I didn't scatter? Then you should have deposited my money with the bankers, and on my return I would have received my money back with interest! Therefore take the talent from him and give it to the one who has ten. For the one who has will be given more, and he will have more than enough. But the one who does not have, even what he has will be taken from him…"

***

Setting Your Goals

This is a very profound story that teaches a very valuable lesson. God has invested a lot into you and He (to put it simply) is looking for a profit! All of the various gifts and talents that you have should be put to good use toward the purpose of creating more of its kind.

If you have the gift of music, you should be producing music. If you're a great chef, you should own a restaurant. If you have a knack for business, you should be an entrepreneur. Whatever it is that you do, you should be busy doing it, and setting each goal so that you end up with more than you started with.

However, too many people are like the unprofitable servant. They bury their talents in self-doubt and excuses, and then have the nerve to pray for millions on top of that. God has already placed inside of you the ingredients necessary for your success. You need only come into the revelation of your purpose, and set your goals accordingly. Even if you just put your resources "in the bank"—that is investing in others to help them accomplish their goals—at the very least, the kingdom will be increased and the Lord will be pleased.

Something else is revealed by the parable of the talents. Notice that the Master gave each servant talents according to their abilities. In other words, the Master was well aware of the level of success that each servant was capable of and assigned resources accordingly. With each talent comes a responsibility to make the most of that talent, and setting the right kind of goal is the key to that success. It would have been nonsensical for the servant with only two talents to try to accomplish the same success as the servant who had been given five.

Yes, we are all equal in God's eyes. But this equality measures the unconditional love that He has for us. Common sense and experience dictate that while God loves us all exactly the same, He did not create us all exactly the same. We're different and we need to capitalize on our differences.

The musician shouldn't be opening a restaurant, no matter how great of an idea it seems to be. He'd do much better opening a jazz café. Meanwhile, the businessman may easily become a multi-millionaire investing in the markets. This wouldn't be surprising because it is apparent that he has a natural talent for dealing with money. And it wouldn't make any sense for the chef to be jealous because his restaurant only profits in the hundred thousands. After all, his gifting is toward *food*, not money.

But now imagine that the musician, the businessman, and the chef all come together to start a national chain of restaurants with live music. With each working according to *his* ability, they're sure to make a dynamic team, each experiencing his own level of personal success. Setting such a goal would definitely be worthwhile and in godly order. They'd all be millionaires.

So, set your goals according to who you are and what you are meant to do. If your vision goes beyond the scope of your ability, don't try to force it. This probably just means that you need to add some people to your team. And until your team arrives, work with what you have and be realistic about what you can accomplish.

Being "realistic" doesn't mean that you squash your dreams and say, "I can't." Being "realistic" means that you understand that life and success is a process. It requires patience, timing, education, and multiple levels of effort depending on what you mean to accomplish.

Say, "I *can* live my dreams" because you can—even if your dream is to be a millionaire. But remember it's not about the millions. It's about purpose. Allow yourself time to mature into your destiny, setting goals that reflect the gifting and calling upon your life.

Chapter 5: Acknowledging the Team

Okay, so you know what your goals are. Now what? How are you going to get there? How do you plan to win? You may feel an impulse to just go out, give it your all and think that you're going to run the whole marathon by yourself...

Warning: that wouldn't be wise.

You may say, "But I'm an excellent runner. I trained myself and everything. I don't need anyone or anything but my own two legs." However, let's say you hurt your leg while running on the track and the paramedics arrive. Or maybe others in the race hoist you up. Even though you don't know these people yet, they're still on your team.

Your team is all around you: someone started the company that bottled your water, another paved the roads, another set the course, and even if no one cheers you on, the host of the marathon will definitely give you grand congratulations when

Acknowledging the Team

you finish the race. These are all members of your team: the support that makes the race possible.

Remember, winning is never a solo act. Therefore, it would be wise to acknowledge your team before you just sprint out. After all, they're the ones that are going to help you get "there," wherever "there" may be for you. Knowing the source of your help prepares you for the tough times ahead, and assures that the goal will be met, even if you fall short at some point.

Yes, you need to *acknowledge* your team. And this is different from *forming* your team. Its one thing to go and pick the "best of the best" team members as this is a separate art in and of itself. But how often do we fail to acknowledge the team already in place? Many times God has already made provisions and allowances for our success in the people around us. Sometimes His choices are even ironic: for the team might not just include allies, but also those that we perceive to be enemies...

Let us consider the story of Joseph found in the book of Genesis, chapters 37 to 50. To summarize:

> Joseph was a 17-year-old boy. He was the youngest of 12 brothers, and the chosen favorite of his father, Jacob, the grandson of Abraham. Jacob loved Joseph so much that he made him a "coat of many colors." This made Joseph's brothers very jealous of him. And it didn't help that Joseph once shared a prophetic dream with them in which everyone in the family bowed to him. Needless to say, the brothers didn't like this one bit...
>
> One day, Jacob sent Joseph out to check on his older brothers who were out feeding the flock. The brothers saw him coming and conspired to kill him. But one brother, Reuben, convinced them not to kill their own "flesh and

blood." So, the others decided to through Joseph into a pit and sell him into slavery instead!

They faked his death by dipping his colorful coat in goat's blood, and told their father that a wild animal had eaten him. Jacob was sorely grieved.

Joseph was then sold to a wealthy military official named Potiphar. Joseph's hard work as a slave found him favor with Potiphar who made him the head steward of his entire estate.

For 10 years everything was fine until Potiphar's wife developed a sexual attraction to Joseph and compelled him to have relations with her. An honorable man, Joseph refused—on multiple occasions—until finally, out of anger, frustration, and embarrassment, she cried rape!

Potiphar threw Joseph in a dungeon. However, God was still with him so that Joseph found favor with the chief of the prison and was made the top prisoner, given special duties over the other prisoners.

Meanwhile, the Pharaoh of Egypt threw his chief cupbearer and baker into the prison. They were given to Joseph's care, and they went on to share frightening dreams that he interpreted by the power of God. As Joseph had prophesied, the baker would be executed, and the cupbearer would be restored to his position in Pharaoh's palace.

Joseph asked the cupbearer to remember him, to ask Pharaoh for his freedom. However, when the cupbearer got back to Pharaoh's place he forgot all about Joseph—for two years, until Pharaoh had a disturbing dream that needed an interpreter. Then the cupbearer remembered Joseph and recommended him to Pharaoh.

Acknowledging the Team

By the power of God, Joseph interpreted Pharaoh's dream to prophesy 7 years of plenty followed by 7 years of famine. Pharaoh took heed and appointed Joseph to the highest rank possible: second in command in charge of preparing for the famine!

Years later during the famine which came to pass, Jacob sent his sons to Egypt to get food. They came before Joseph and he recognized them, but they didn't recognize him. In a strange plot twist (probably trying to teach them a lesson), he accused them of being spies, and wouldn't take their word that they were not until they brought their youngest brother, Benjamin, back to him. He locked up one brother, Simeon, for collateral. They went back to tell Jacob.

Angry and hungry, Jacob took his sons back to Egypt to settle the matter. Upon their return, Joseph was so happy to see all of them, especially the youngest Benjamin. Eventually, he revealed himself and forgave his brothers. The family bowed to him in gratitude, fulfilling the prophecy of his childhood dream. The whole family permanently moved to Egypt. They wanted for nothing and lived happily ever after.

***

When we look at the story of Joseph, most of us would consider his brothers to be his worst enemies. They didn't like him. They threw him in a pit, and sold him into slavery. Once Joseph had been sold into slavery, we would also consider his enemy to be the slave master, Potiphar, or the chief of the prison, where he was thrown into captivity after he refused to sleep with Potiphar's wife.

However, all of these people were members of Joseph's *team*. Yes, the brothers, Potiphar, and the chief of the prison. The reason for this is that without the brothers, and the others mentioned, Joseph would never have reached his full potential and destiny as second in command over the land of Egypt. He could never have applied his anointing of dream interpretation—an anointing that saved an entire kingdom from a devastating famine that came upon the land.

So we see, even though he was faced with great obstacles brought upon him by those that treated him wrong, he was still able to come out on top. Joseph refused to give into the pressure. He didn't attack his enemies—but rather used the attack of his enemies to catapult himself forward!

In other words, in this case, Joseph was the *arrow* and his enemies were the *bow*. In your life, you may also find that your enemies are the bow that will propel you into your future and destiny.

Joseph acknowledged God; he acknowledged the call that was upon his life; and then he acknowledged his team. He didn't look at his circumstance as the thing that would hold him back. Ultimately, his trying circumstance worked to his advantage and assisted him greatly in regard to obtaining a prosperous future and reaching an outstanding life achievement. Through it all, Joseph fulfilled the old adage, "When life gives you lemons make lemonade," and so it should be in your own life.

Acknowledge all the factors that are preparing you for who you're going to be. Never look at anything as happenstance, coincidental, or simply out of place. Everything in your life is there for a reason. Every obstacle or setback that you're being faced with has the power to make you better if you choose to see it that way—if you choose to acknowledge that everyone in your life is on your *team*.

Now, this is not to say that we don't have enemies. This doesn't mean that you would enjoy being thrown into a pit, or accused of rape, or that you will always find happiness in the prisons of the various circumstances that you will encounter throughout life. However, with the help of God, you shall be delivered from every prison and you shall face your accusers.

And in that moment you will have forgiveness in your heart because you will see what God has done *for you—through them*. You'll understand that what the devil meant for evil, God completely turned around and caused that particular test or hardship to work out for your good!

The Bible says that, "...we know that all things work together for good to them that love God, to them who are the called according to his purpose." (Romans 8:28) And while some theologians have debated the exact meaning of this text, I believe that most would agree that it is applicable to my point: that good comes to those that love God and live toward the fulfillment of godly purposes.

Have you acknowledged all the things working together to help you fulfill your purpose?

Granted, most of your team won't be comprised of enemies. However, they may still be unbeknownst to you, sometimes the most unlikely of heroes.

Recall that the cupbearer was only in Joseph's life for a brief moment. And yet, they proved to be valuable teammates in the long run. Joseph cared for the cupbearer and interpreted his dream while in prison. This ultimately prepared the cupbearer to be restored back to his royal position in Pharaoh's palace. In turn, even though it took a while, the cupbearer was able to recommend Joseph to Pharaoh, a referral that definitely resulted in Joseph being promoted to his God-ordained destiny as second in command over all of Egypt.

Imagine that: from the *prison* to the *palace*!

Is there someone in your life who has played a small but significant role? Or maybe it's a really big role carried out behind the scenes, and either way you've failed to acknowledge them. Often they are silently (or not so silently) crying out like Joseph did to the cupbearer, "Remember me." Even if they always say, "Oh, its no big deal," you know how much they *really* mean. Make sure that they know it: a simple "thank you" or act of appreciation can go a long way. Let them know how much you value their contribution to your success.

Maybe that "hero" is a parent that you've taken for granted, or a co-worker who's always doing you little favors; perhaps, a teacher that helped to shape your thinking, or an oddball friend who's been there through thick and thin. It's been said that, "No man is an island," and this saying is true. We're all in this together. Acknowledge the people around you and the multiple ways that they affect your life.

And above all, don't forget to acknowledge God. The Bible says, "In all your ways acknowledge him, and he shall direct your paths." (Proverbs 3:6) The guidance and gifting of God contributed to Joseph's winning in life more than anything else. No doubt, Joseph was fully aware of and revered the blessing of the Lord in his life, especially when it came to the gift of dream interpretation, "...Joseph answered Pharaoh, saying, 'It is not in me: God shall give Pharaoh an answer of peace.'" (Genesis 41:16)

Likewise, it is important to realize that when it comes to the decisive moments of your life, the Word of God is always there to provide the "answer of peace."

So, as you prepare to run life's marathon, drink the free-flowing life-giving water of the Word of God daily. Let the Word refresh you! It is the only thing that will consistently prepare you for what's ahead on the road to winning in life. There is no reason to be apprehensive about your future or plagued with doubts concerning your destiny. God has placed you on a winning team! Make sure you acknowledge it!

Chapter 6:
3 Strategies for Winning

Winning is a strategic art. It is the art of planning the most expedient and effective course to victory. One great strategy for winning in life is to examine what others have done—their methods, successes and their failures—and see if you can, by adopting or improving upon their methods, replicate their successes while avoiding their failures.

In Numbers 13, we find the children of Israel preparing to possess the land of Canaan, the "Promised Land." Having delivered them from slavery in Egypt, now God is preparing them for the next level of victory. He commands Moses to send out scouts (one from each of the twelve tribes) to evaluate the territory and the inhabitants thereof. They eventually return with a report, bringing back fruit from the land that "flows with milk and honey." It was everything they could have ever wanted…

But did they possess it? Did they *win*?

Let's take a look at the story to see what becomes of their journey into the Promised Land. By thus we shall learn from their experiences. And with due diligence, we will be able to apply the truths of such lessons learned to our own lives. We shall witness the promise and the pitfalls, points of failure, and how to position ourselves for success... We will learn God-given strategies for wining in life.

Numbers 13

And the LORD spoke to Moses, saying, "Send men to spy out the land of Canaan, which I am giving to the children of Israel; from each tribe of their fathers you shall send a man, every one a leader among them."

Then Moses sent them to spy out the land of Canaan, and said to them, "Go up this way into the South, and go up to the mountains, and see what the land is like: whether the people who dwell in it are strong or weak, few or many; whether the land they dwell in is good or bad; whether the cities they inhabit are like camps or strongholds; whether the land is rich or poor; and whether there are forests there or not. Be of good courage. And bring some of the fruit of the land." Now the time was the season of the first ripe grapes.

So they went up and spied out the land from the Wilderness of Zin as far as Rehob, near the entrance of Hamath. And they went up through the South and came to Hebron; Ahiman, Sheshai, and Talmai, the descendants of Anak, were there. (Now Hebron was built seven years before Zoan in Egypt.) Then they came to the Valley of Eshcol, and there cut down a branch with one cluster of grapes; they carried it between two of them on a pole. They also brought some of the pomegranates and figs. The place was called the Valley of Eshcol, because of the cluster which the men of Israel cut down there. And they returned from spying out the land after forty days.

Now they departed and came back to Moses and Aaron and all the congregation of the children of Israel in the Wilderness of Paran, at Kadesh; they brought back word to them and to all the congregation, and showed them the fruit of the land. Then they told him, and said: "We went to the land where you sent us. It truly flows with milk and honey, and this is its fruit. Nevertheless the people who dwell in the land are strong; the cities are fortified and very large; moreover we saw the descendants of Anak there. The Amalekites dwell in the land of the South; the Hittites, the Jebusites, and the Amorites dwell in the mountains; and the Canaanites dwell by the sea and along the banks of the Jordan."

Then Caleb quieted the people before Moses, and said, "Let us go up at once and take possession, for we are well able to overcome it."

But the men who had gone up with him said, "We are not able to go up against the people, for they are stronger than we." And they gave the children of Israel a bad report of the land which they had spied out, saying, "The land through which we have gone as spies is a land that devours its inhabitants, and all the people whom we saw in it are men of great stature. There we saw the giants (the descendants of Anak came from the giants); and we were like grasshoppers in our own sight, and so we were in their sight…" (NKJV)

***

So, what should we take from this story?

Well, the children of Israel *did* eventually possess the land of Canaan, but not *here*. It would take 40 years of roaming in the wilderness before all of the doubters and naysayers died off. God would lead the *next* generation to victory. In fact, Caleb and Joshua (Moses' right-hand men) were the only two from the former generation that actually made it into the Promised Land—not even Moses went!

Now you may be thinking, "What went wrong?" But before we learn the answer to this question, let's examine how it was supposed to go and how God intended for them to make it right. No doubt, God had given them everything that they needed to succeed, starting with the following *3 Strategies for Winning in Life.*

Strategy #1: Know and Explore Your Goals

The first thing that God commanded them to do was to survey the land of Canaan. We've talked about setting goals according to your calling. Yes, indeed, God called Israel to possess the Promised Land. Howbeit, it is entirely impossible to set a goal—to nail a target—if you can't see it.

Usually we have some image in our minds of what we want to accomplish. But this doesn't mean that we actually *know* what we're dealing with or even how to obtain it. Therefore, it is important to get a visual of what you want out of life. Though it has a place, imagination is not enough. You need to literally see what you're going after. And for the great God that He is, if you seek, God will always show it to you.

Years ago, when my wife and I first got married, we didn't have a lot of money. Yet, this didn't stop us from traveling around to look at beautiful homes in nice neighborhoods. We drove a brand new *Vette*—a blue '86 Chevy Chevette! We were very appreciative of God's blessings and we were sure that He was preparing us for bigger and better things. At the time we were just living in a small duplex. But, eventually, we moved into our own home, quite comparable to the homes that we used to dream about! Glory to God!

It all started with a visual: a vision. Because we had seen it, we were able to go after the very thing that God had shown us.

"Where there is no vision, the people perish..." (Proverbs 29:18) Of all the senses, vision is perhaps the most crucial for navigating unknown territory. If you want to accomplish something that you've never accomplished before in the will of God, you need to get a clear vision of where God is taking you.

Without a vision, you and your team will be in danger of lacking the inspiration and guidance necessary to achieve your goals in life. In other words, without a vision the hope of accomplishing your dreams will "perish" because you won't even know how to go about possessing the very thing that is in store for you.

Do you know what God has in store for you—in this life?

Numbers 13:23 says that, "...they came to the Valley of Eshcol, and there cut down a branch with one cluster of grapes; they carried it between two of them on a pole."

It took *two* men to carry *one* cluster of grapes from the land. Man, those must have been some serious grapes! Truly, the Promised Land did flow with milk and honey. It was a land of Prosperity. And the children of Israel would have never known what God had prepared for them had they not went out to explore it.

God has great things in store for you. Recall that His promises are "Yes and Amen." The Bible says that He is able to "do exceeding abundantly above all that we ask or think, according to the power that works in us." (Ephesians 3:20) God is able to exceed even your greatest thoughts of abundance and prosperity, according to the power that He has already invested in you. Still, you will never know what you can do by His power if you don't explore the land.

Exploration requires both courage and initiative. To explore, you must step out of your comfort zone and actually go out into unknown territory. And you never know what you'll find...

The investigative journey into the land of Canaan revealed more than juicy grapes. It also made Israel aware of the formidable inhabitants of the land. Surviving as a spy among them was no easy task. But based on the fact that they were able to successfully infiltrate the enemy's territory, undetected, we know that God could have easily given them the same advantage in battle. God had been protecting them all along, and He would have continued to do so.

Know that God will go with you into the land of Promise, even if it's currently inhabited by what you perceive to be giants. No matter how great the obstacles may seem, it is important to trust that God will never put you in a position that you can't handle. Remember Jesus said, "Lo, I am with you always, even unto the end of the world." (Matthew 28:20) God is always with you, so there's no reason to be afraid of anything. Go ahead, launch out into the deep!

Exploration also requires patience and trust in God. I am reminded of a story in which Jesus taught the disciples a very valuable lesson about patience and trust in Him, which is needed when exploring goals. It is found in John 21.

John 21

After these things Jesus showed Himself again to the disciples at the Sea of Tiberias, and in this way He showed Himself: Simon Peter, Thomas called the Twin, Nathanael of Cana in Galilee, the sons of Zebedee, and two others of His disciples were together. Simon Peter said to them, "I am going fishing."

They said to him, "We are going with you also." They went out and immediately got into the boat, and that night they caught nothing. But when the morning had now come, Jesus stood on the shore; yet the disciples did not know that it was Jesus. Then Jesus said to them, "children, have you any food?"

They answered Him, "No."

And He said to them, "Cast the net on the right side of the boat, and you will find some." So they cast, and now they were not able to draw it in because of the multitude of fish.

Therefore that disciple whom Jesus loved said to Peter, "It is the Lord!" Now when Simon Peter heard that it was the Lord, he put on his outer garment (for he had removed it), and plunged into the sea. But the other disciples came in the little boat (for they were not far from land, but about two hundred cubits), dragging the net with fish. Then, as soon as they had come to land, they saw a fire of coals there, and fish laid on it, and bread. Jesus said to them, "Bring some of the fish which you have just caught."

Simon Peter went up and dragged the net to land, full of large fish, one hundred and fifty-three; and although there were so many, the net was not broken. Jesus said to them,

"Come and eat breakfast." Yet none of the disciples dared ask Him, "Who are You?"—knowing that it was the Lord. Jesus then came and took the bread and gave it to them, and likewise the fish. (NKJV)

***

The disciples had been working all night as a team toward a very specific goal: to catch fish. They were just about ready to give up, having caught nothing. When Jesus came along and instructed them to try again they could have easily said, "No thanks, we've already tried that!"

How often do we make this mistake?

How often do we ignore the Word of the Lord because we've "heard it before" or "been there, and done that"? When God gives you instruction, you need to move out on it without hesitation. After all, who knows how to accomplish your goals best besides the One that made you to accomplish them?

This is not to say that you haven't already been working hard or that your previous efforts are meaningless. However, it is to say that the quantity of your efforts should never be used as an excuse to ignore the Word of the Lord. Work is simply a part of the winning equation. Therefore, it is important to remain busy at work doing and exploring those things that God has already instilled in you, until He sends further instruction.

Don't be discouraged. You may have to work for a while. But often the knowledge will come *in the midst* of your work and explorations. Before you know it, Jesus will appear with the very revelation that you seek as you're earnestly seeking to find it. It just takes patience and trust.

Gaining the knowledge and experience necessary to accomplish your goal of winning in life won't likely come all at once. Sometimes, you may have to "work all night." You may have to go back and rediscover things that you thought you already knew especially if you didn't get the full revelation the first time around.

The leaders of Israel had gone spying for 40 days and, except for Caleb, not a single one of them returned with a full understanding of what God meant for them: they were not convinced of what they could have or what had been placed inside of them. Instead of renewing their thoughts and reflecting on all the good things that God had shown them during the exploration, they got caught up in fear...

Remember that exploration requires courage. So, don't be afraid. Don't be afraid of what God is showing you. If He's showed it to you, it's for you to see. And it's yours to have, according to His will and by His power.

Don't be afraid of being overloaded, overwhelmed, or overtaken. Remember, God will never put you in a position that you can't handle. You'll receive a multitude of fish, but your net will not break! If you find that the cluster of grapes is too big for you to carry alone, look around for that team member already in place, ready to help you receive your blessing. And even if you have to face the "giant" inhabitants of the land, God is well able to deliver them into your hands too!

Go ahead, launch out into the deep!

Don't be afraid to try again.

Sometimes, we do fail. Sometimes we get it wrong, or maybe the original timing just wasn't right. Either way, you have to trust that it's not over until God says it's over. The disciples had to trust Jesus when He said, "Try again." Even if you think you've explored all of your options, don't resist the Word of the Lord to "try again."

Maybe you'll have to go back to school, or reapply for that loan. Maybe you'll require additional training for the task ahead or maybe you'll have to face your greatest fear once again. Whatever the case, as you approach the next hurdle in life, resist all self-doubt and forget about past failures. If God says go, go! Whatever it is that you have to do, do it. And, with the help of the Lord, you are guaranteed to succeed.

In the end, God desires that you (and He) would enjoy the profit of your abundance. God wants to be glorified through your life. And so you need an understanding of the vision that He has for you. Know and explore your goals with vision, courage, initiative, patience and trust. Embrace the possibilities. Not only will this inspire you toward your goals, but it will also prepare you for the battle to seize it ahead. Which brings us to the next point—

Strategy #2: Know Your Enemy; Know the Opposition

It is virtually impossible to fight your enemy if you don't know who or *what* you are fighting. Undoubtedly, getting to know the opposition is the first step toward understanding how it can be successfully overcome.

When the children of Israel went to spy out the land of Canaan, the nature and *stature* of the inhabitants were some of the main things that they observed. They said, "We are not able to go up against the people, for they are stronger than we…The land through which we have gone as spies is a land that devours its inhabitants, and all the people whom we saw in it are men of great stature. There we saw the giants…and we were like grasshoppers in our own sight, and so we were in their sight..." (Numbers 13:31-33)

The spies observed that their enemy was of great stature, and prone to "devouring." Truly, they had sized up the enemy, and now they were afraid. However, the mistake was not in sizing up the enemy, but in adding *fear* to the equation.

Let's take their word for it and imagine that the inhabitants really were flesh-eating giants. So what? The bigger they are, the harder they fall, right? It is important to understand that getting to know your enemy has nothing to do with being afraid of him.

After you size up the enemy (i.e. acknowledge the challenge before you), don't be intimidated by his size. Else, if you're not careful, your greatest enemy won't be the opposition on the outside, but the self-doubt on the inside. Don't mess around and hand over the victory before the fight even starts on account of some inferiority complex.

Remember greater is He that is in you, than He that is in the world. (1 John 4:4)

As a child of God, sayings like "I'm just a little grasshopper," or "I'm inferior," shouldn't even be a part of your vernacular. At all times, your attitude should be, "I am who God says I am, and I can do whatever He has empowered me to do."

What are you so afraid of?

F.E.A.R. (False Evidence Appearing Real) is the exact opposite of faith, or—better said—its faith in the *wrong* thing. Your faith should be in God, not your enemy. While you're getting to know your opposition, never forget that you *know* your God!

Whose report are you going to believe?

The enemy will always try to get you caught up in fear of who he is and what *might* do. And if you give into the fear, you've lost the war before the first battle even starts. The enemy knows that if he can get you to quit or forfeit outright, there's no chance of his defeat. Obviously, he doesn't want to fight you and your God, so he employs the tactic of fear.

The Bible says that, "Lest Satan should get an advantage of us…we are not ignorant of his devices." (2 Corinthians 2:11) In other words, we are not unaware of his schemes: the continual plot to cloud our minds with ignorance, hasty judgments, erroneous conclusions, fear, and doubt concerning the power of God that works in us.

With God on your team, there is no reason to feel inferior or to be afraid. James 4:7 says, "Submit yourselves therefore to God. Resist the devil, and he will flee from you." Keep this in mind: submit yourself to the commandment of the Lord and meditate on His promises; go in *His* strength and *His* might, you'll have all your enemies running for cover!

At the parting of the Red Sea, Moses encouraged the children of Israel, "Fear not, stand still, and see the salvation of the LORD, which he will show to you to day: for the Egyptians whom you have seen to day, you shall see them again no more for ever." (Exodus 14:13, KJV)

God had already demonstrated His ability to defeat formidable foes when He defeated the army of the Egyptians. Surely, He was well-able to handle the Sons of Anak (the giants). When God sent the children of Israel to survey the land and to get to know the enemy, it was not for them to become fearful. Rather, it was that they might see and assess the land that God had empowered them to conquer, and the enemy that He would surely help them overcome.

Again, getting to know your enemy has nothing to do with being afraid of him. It has all to do with coming to understand yourself in the light of God's calling upon your life, and therefore cultivating your strengths to combat your enemy's weaknesses.

And yes, every enemy has a weakness. Didn't young David slay Goliath? (Samuel 17) David knocked him out with a slingshot right between the eyes, and cut off Goliath's head—with Goliath's sword! If one young man accomplished this by the power of God, imagine what the armies of Israel could have done had they stepped out on God's Word.

Knowing your enemy means coming to know the truth about him, not to be confused with your imagination or opinion. Don't assume that your enemy sees you as inferior. Many times, it's the exact opposite. While you're sizing him up, he's sizing you up too. Often enough, he is more afraid than you think. But you'll never see the fear in his eyes, until you *look* him in the eyes and say, "Satan, the Lord rebuke you in the Name of Jesus!" Trust the Lord to lead you into victory.

Strategy #3: Get Confirmation of Gods' Promises

Nothing helps your confidence in God more than getting a confirmation of His promises. Remember those grapes? The cluster of grapes was Israel's confirmation that the land of Canaan was in fact the Promised Land, a land that flowed with milk and honey, a land of Prosperity.

The cluster of grapes was there to inspire them. It was a *visual* of what God had promised them: to deliver them from the bondage of Egypt into a land of their own. It was bigger than just coming out of the wilderness and finding a place to dwell.

It was about restoration...

Have you ever wondered how the children of Israel ended up slaves in Egypt in the first place?

If you recall, Jacob (also named *Israel*) moved his family (11 sons and their families) to Egypt to rendezvous with his son Joseph. Over the course of many years in Egypt, the descendants of Jacob all grew and prospered to become a great nation: the children of Israel. They grew so strong that the Egyptians perceived them to be a threat and moved to make them slaves to keep them under control. (Read Exodus 1)

Their prosperity was stripped from them. And now, here at the gates of the Promised Land, this was their opportunity to get that prosperity back. However, all those years of slavery had prevailed in their minds and they were held back by a slave mentality—that, "I'm a little grasshopper" type of thinking.

You see, it can be mentally hard to win a fight, if you've lost the same fight before. If you're use to losing, you tend to see yourself as a loser. And this will inevitably cause you to second guess the investment God's placed inside of you and the blessings that He has in store. Worst, it may even cause you to second guess your faith in God Himself!

God is not one of the "Egyptians." He has no ill-intention toward us; His thoughts of us are not evil.

Jeremiah 29:11 encourages us, "For I know the thoughts that I think toward you, saith the LORD, thoughts of peace, and not of evil, to give you an expected end." Many times, as we go through the trials of life, we are tempted to believe that God has forgotten about us, or—worst yet—that He is behind the suffering, a suffering to which there will be no end. But nothing could be further from the truth.

God has an *expected end* for you, one of peace and prosperity, void of suffering. Do not hesitate to take Him at his Word and seek confirmation of His promises. Renew your faith in Him for He shall deliver you from the bondage of your slavery (whatever it is) and shall bring you into the land that He's promised you!

But you have to believe. Faith is the key to your success in Him! You won't move out on God's Word if you don't believe His Word and that His promises are true. And we see that this was the primary issue with Israel.

To answer the earlier question, that's what went wrong. Even though they had been given strategies for winning in life, without activated faith, their works toward success fell dead. (James 2:17). The former generation did not inherit the Promised Land because they lacked faith.

Let's avoid falling into that same pit. In the next chapter we shall examine *3 Keys to Activating Your Faith*...

Chapter 7:
3 Keys to Activating Your Faith

The Bible says, "Now faith is the substance of things hoped for, the evidence of things not seen." (Hebrews 11:1)

In other words, faith is the product of our expectations. It is the inspiration that moves us into action toward victory, even when it may appear that the odds are against us. Corinthians 12:9 lets us know that faith is a gift of the Spirit. It is literally a gift from God: one that we can have confidence in, as God has dealt each of us a measure of it. (Romans 12:3)

As children of the King, we must live by faith, incorporating it into all aspects our lives. Romans 10:6 lets us know that, "For therein is the righteousness of God revealed from *faith* to *faith*: as it is written, The just shall live by faith." To live by faith means to be *active* in faith, making the most of the measure of faith that God has deposited into your Spirit. And with the resource of faith, you can accomplish natural and supernatural successes of all sorts—you can win in life despite difficult odds.

Yes, faith can even move mountains. However, you might not start out moving mountains. (Remember, God will never put you in a situation that you're not prepared to handle.) You may have to start by moving a molehill first. And then, maybe move up to a larger hill—and then a mountain. In this, it is important to understand that, like winning in life, faith is a process: a daily walk with God.

As you grow in God, each of your life's experiences will help to develop your faith and confidence in God's ability to work mightily through you. Therefore, as you approach each new challenge in life, remember how far God has brought you. And as you reflect on His goodness, you are sure to find the guidance and strength needed to resolutely face the challenges ahead—even if the challenge is a Goliath!

By the time we arrived to Numbers 13, God had done many awesome things for the children of Israel:

He had strengthened and preserved them in bondage, He had raised up Moses to lead them out of slavery; He had protected them from the ten plagues; He had delivered them from the hardened heart of Pharaoh and brought them out of the land of Egypt with great riches; He had parted the Red Sea so that they crossed over on dry land and defeated Pharaoh's armies by drowning them in the sea; and finally He ushered the children of Israel to the gates of the Promised Land.

God had taken them from *faith* to *faith*—experience after experience, showing them His great power with the primary intent of increasing their confidence in Him. In all these things, God had given them total victory over the greatest enemy they had ever faced.

And yet, they had a problem visualizing success against their new enemy in the land of Canaan. They cried out for fear of the giant inhabitants of the land, "We are not able to go up against the people, for they are stronger than we...We were like grasshoppers in our own sight, and so we were in their sight..." (Numbers 13:31, 33)

Despite everything that God had done for them, they lacked faith. Not only did they lack faith in the promise of God to deliver the land to them, but they lacked faith in themselves and what God had invested in them from the very beginning...

Faith is crucial for godly success in life. The Bible says that by it, "...the elders obtained a good report..." (Hebrews 11:2) The Bible reports that the children of Israel had a long history of faith-filled patriarchs who had accomplished many successes of biblical proportion, winning every time by the power of God.

Hebrews 11 goes on to testify that:

By faith Abraham obeyed when he was called to go out to the place which he would receive as an inheritance. And he went out, not knowing where he was going. By faith he dwelt in the land of promise as in a foreign country, dwelling in tents with Isaac and Jacob, the heirs with him of the same promise; for he waited for the city which has foundations, whose builder and maker is God.

By faith Sarah herself also received strength to conceive seed, and she bore a child when she was past the age, because she judged Him faithful who had promised. Therefore from one man, and him as good as dead, were born as many as the stars of the sky in multitude— innumerable as the sand which is by the seashore.

By faith Abraham, when he was tested, offered up Isaac, and he who had received the promises offered up his only begotten son, of whom it was said, "In Isaac your seed shall be called," concluding that God was able to raise him up, even from the dead, from which he also received him in a figurative sense.

By faith Isaac blessed Jacob and Esau concerning things to come.

By faith Jacob, when he was dying, blessed each of the sons of Joseph, and worshiped, leaning on the top of his staff.

By faith Joseph, when he was dying, made mention of the departure of the children of Israel, and gave instructions concerning his bones.

By faith Moses, when he was born, was hidden three months by his parents, because they saw he was a beautiful child; and they were not afraid of the king's command.

By faith Moses, when he became of age, refused to be called the son of Pharaoh's daughter, choosing rather to suffer affliction with the people of God than to enjoy the passing pleasures of sin, esteeming the reproach of Christ greater riches than the treasures in Egypt; for he looked to the reward.

By faith he forsook Egypt, not fearing the wrath of the king; for he endured as seeing Him who is invisible. By faith he kept the Passover and the sprinkling of blood, lest he who destroyed the firstborn should touch them.

By faith they passed through the Red Sea as by dry land, whereas the Egyptians, attempting to do so, were drowned. (NKJV)

***

Israel had a powerful testimony indeed. God had shown forth His power on their behalf throughout the whole span of their history. He had led Abraham toward the fulfillment of a great promise to be the father of many nations. He had set Joseph in a seat of power and given children of Israel prosperity in the Land of Egypt. And finally, He had delivered them from slavery in Egypt—and all this by faith!

However, the toll of slavery had had a devastating effect on the generation that surveyed the land of Canaan: the generation that would have inherited the Promised Land, had they only believed. What a shame: they did not enter in the Promised Land because they had no faith.

Again, faith is crucial for godly success. Without it, you will not obtain a "good report" because you will be too afraid to step out on God's report (that is, His Word) to meet your destiny and fulfill your dreams. In order to accomplish your goals, faith must be alive and active in your life.

You must have a *living* faith.

Therefore, let us examine *3 Keys to Activating Your Faith* so that you will be able to cross the finish line when God ushers you to the gates of your Promised Land.

Key #1: Silence the Crowd

When the leaders from the twelve tribes of Israel returned from surveying the Land, all but one came back with a negative report concerning the prospect of conquest.

The Bible says that, "...Caleb quieted the people before Moses, and said, 'Let us go up at once and take possession, for we are well able to overcome it.'" (Numbers 13:30)

However, even though Caleb believed that Israel could conquer, the men who had gone up with him said, "We are not able to go up against the people, for they are stronger than we." And they gave the children of Israel a bad report of the land which they had spied out, saying, "The land through which we have gone as spies is a land that devours its inhabitants..." (Numbers 12:31-32)

Truly, this was a very bad report. And unfortunately, the children of Israel chose to believe it.

Why is it that we are so inclined to believe the "bad report"? Why are we so inclined to believe the discouraging things that people say, when they tell us what we can't do?

Perhaps, you've received a negative report on the job: "You'll never get a raise." Perhaps, you've received a negative report from the doctor: "You have cancer." Maybe they said that you don't have what it takes to finish school, or that your business will never be successful. Whoever *they* are and whatever they said, it is important to understand that when faced with the choice to believe a negative report or God's report, always choose to believe God's report.

And often this means that you have to silence the crowd.

Before the negative reports even came in, Caleb silenced the crowd. And in that silence, he prepared the people to hear the

Word of the Lord, which reechoed the winner's attitude, "We can do it!" No doubt, Caleb was well aware of what the other spies believed and what their opinions were. Still, Caleb had faith that God would give them the victory. Undoubtedly, they had all assessed many challenges while surveying the land. However, it didn't make a difference what was behind them; Caleb was convinced that they could move forward.

The Apostle Paul said, "...this one thing I do, forgetting those things which are behind, and reaching forth unto those things which are before, I press toward the mark for the prize of the high calling of God in Christ Jesus." (Philippians 3:13-14)

Put all doubt behind you and press toward the mark of your calling in Christ Jesus. Silence the crowd of haters and naysayers and know that God has called you to be a winner! No matter what the challenge, regardless of the opposition, know that God is well-able to lead you into the Promised Land. Keep your eyes on the prize and silence the crowd.

You'll never possess the Promised Land as long as you're paralyzed by false evidence appearing real in negative reports coming from every other direction. Silence the crowd!

And sometimes, the crowd can be your own mind.

The Bible instructs us to cast down imaginations and every "high thing" that exalts itself against the knowledge of God, and bring into captivity every thought to the obedience of Christ. (2 Corinthians 10:5) Yes, even your own thoughts must be subject to the word of the Lord. Don't even allow your own thoughts to steer you in the wrong direction.

Romans 10:17 lets us know that, "...faith comes by hearing, and hearing by the word of God." What you hear and allow to be fed into your spirit will have a direct effect on your faith.

Winning in Life

Therefore, it is important to meditate only on God's word and His promises. If God says it, that settles it. Period.

If God says that He's going to prosper you on your job, look out for a raise. If God says that you can be healed of cancer, expect you're healing! If God says you can finish school, or fulfill your dream of owning a prosperous business go make it happen! It doesn't make a difference who says the opposite—be it friends, family, your enemy, or your own mind—silence the crowd and step out on His Word.

Remember, with God on your team, you have nothing to lose. Whatever the challenge, you're well-able to overcome it. Your enemy's only hope of victory is that you would be defeated in your mind. Therefore, he sends out all kinds of negative reports in an attempt to get you caught up in fear and confusion. But it doesn't make a difference how big and bad that the enemy says he is. The devil is a liar! He's only coming after your faith. Activate your faith in God by telling the devil to shut up!

Which brings us to the next point—

Key #2: Never Magnify the Opposition or Problem

"We looked liked grasshoppers in our own sight, and so we were in their sight..." What a defeated thing to say!

Often obstacles will appear much bigger and more problematic than they actually are. This isn't to say that you shouldn't assess the challenge at hand or underestimate its magnitude. However, you should never *magnify* the problem. In other words, don't make it out to be bigger than it is. Don't exalt it.

King David said, "O magnify the LORD with me, and let us exalt his name together." (Psalm 34:3) Magnify the *Lord*, not the problem. Exalt *His* name—not the name of poverty, the name of that sickness, or the Goliath's that may be inhabiting your Promised Land. Have faith in God and the fact that He has empowered you to defeat everything that is not like Him.

Having faith in God means having faith in what He has placed inside of you. Sometimes you can magnify the problem just by seeing yourself in the wrong way, that you're too small to accomplish the task at hand.

Remember that the value that you place on yourself will be the value that others place on you. People will define you the way that you define yourself. Know that God sees a winner in you and it is important that you see the same. Never make the mistake of underestimating yourself as this is just as bad as—if not worst than—overestimating the enemy.

How do you *really* see yourself?

It's not just enough to say that you're a child of the King, you have to believe it. It's not just enough to think that you can be prosperous or healed of sickness, you have to believe it. You'll never defeat Goliath, if you don't believe that you can take him down. Even if the problem is bigger than you, you have to say like Paul said, "I can do all things through Christ which strengthens me." (Philippians 4:13)

Activate your faith by taking on the mind of Christ; believe that you are what God says you are, and that you can do what He says you can do! And for every word of opposition, and every problem making too much noise, silence the crowd!

I'm reminded of the time when Jesus calmed the raging sea in Mark 4:35-41:

...On the same day, when evening had come, He said to them, "Let us cross over to the other side." Now when they had left the multitude, they took Him along in the boat as He was. And other little boats were also with Him. And a great windstorm arose, and the waves beat into the boat, so that it was already filling. But He was in the stern, asleep on a pillow. And they awoke Him and said to Him, "Teacher, do you not care that we are perishing?"

Then He arose and rebuked the wind, and said to the sea, "Peace, be still!" And the wind ceased and there was a great calm. But He said to them, "Why are you so fearful? How is it that you have no faith?" And they feared exceedingly, and said to one another, "Who can this be, that even the wind and the sea obey Him!" (NKJV)

***

In this story, the disciples thought they were going to die, and they questioned whether or not Jesus even cared. While the waves were violently beating against the boat, Jesus was stilled away, resting in the power of the Almighty. But instead of following the example of Jesus, the disciples decided to magnify the problem in the storm. They cried, "Teacher, do you not care that we are perishing?"

It is God's desire that you would *prosper*, not perish. Yet, even with this knowledge, how often do we doubt God's good intention toward us? How often do we give into the howling winds of life, "You ain't gonna make it."

Jesus easily rebuked the wind, and posed a simple question: Where's your faith?

On another occasion, Jesus met the disciples on the sea. And an amazing thing happened. Matthew 14:22-33 reads as follows:

> Immediately Jesus made His disciples get into the boat and go before Him to the other side, while He sent the multitudes away. And when He had sent the multitudes away, He went up on the mountain by Himself to pray. Now when evening came, He was alone there. But the boat was now in the middle of the sea, tossed by the waves, for the wind was contrary.
>
> Now in the fourth watch of the night Jesus went to them, walking on the sea. And when the disciples saw Him walking on the sea, they were troubled, saying, "It is a ghost!" And they cried out for fear.
>
> But immediately Jesus spoke to them, saying, "Be of good cheer! It is I; do not be afraid."
>
> And Peter answered Him and said, "Lord, if it is You, command me to come to You on the water."
>
> So He said, "Come." And when Peter had come down out of the boat, he walked on the water to go to Jesus. But when he saw that the wind was boisterous, he was afraid; and beginning to sink he cried out, saying, "Lord, save me!"
>
> And immediately Jesus stretched out His hand and caught him, and said to him, "O you of little faith, why did you doubt?" And when they got into the boat, the wind ceased.
>
> Then those who were in the boat came and worshiped Him, saying, "Truly You are the Son of God." (NJKV)

Winning in Life

***

Peter said, "Lord, if it is You, command me to come to You on the water." Many times we have heard the word of the Lord, having received a clear vision and a profound understanding of where He desires to take us.

And just like Peter, we'll start off running the race, doing fine, and gliding over the waters of life, defying the odds. But as soon as things get a little rougher than we expected them to (usually just before the finish line where we would meet Jesus and destiny) we begin to listen to the wrong voice. We start listening to the voice in the winds of troubling circumstances or the voice of self-doubt and inevitably we begin to sink.

But God is faithful, and always there, an ever-present help in the time of trouble. And in time of uncertainty, we need only call upon the name of Jesus and reach out for His unchanging hand!

The amazing thing is that even though Peter magnified the problems, it didn't change the fact that Jesus was still bigger than the problem. Hebrews 13:5 lets us know that He will never leave us or forsake us. Even when we fall short of His calling, He still has a vested interest in picking us up.

Aren't you glad that Jesus is on your team? And just as He asked Peter, He is asking you, "Why would you ever doubt me?"

The word *doubt* literally denotes double-mindedness. Doubt is the product of indecision and confusion concerning which is the bigger of two or more opposing sides.

Which is bigger: God or the problem?

Doubt has no place in the life of a Christian, and usually it only comes when you magnify the problem. A double-minded man is unstable in all his ways. (James 1:8) He is like a wave of the sea, driven by the wind and tossed about. (James 1:6) Fortunately, this instability can be defeated by faith; therefore, activate your faith. Never magnify the opposition or the problem. Rather, choose to magnify the power of God.

Key #3: Maintain a Positive Attitude

We read about the winner's attitude in Chapter 3. Once you've acquired the winner's attitude, it is important to maintain it with a positive attitude. Doing so will ensure that your faith remains healthy in the joy of the Lord.

The joy of the Lord is your strength. (Nehemiah 8:10) This means that you should never let the events of the day determine your level of happiness or confidence. Rather, this should be affirmed by your relationship with God, looking forward to the wonderful promises that He has in store for you.

I can hear the Spirit of the Lord encouraging us with these words, "…delight yourself in the LORD; and I will cause you to ride upon the high places of the earth, and feed you with the heritage of Jacob your father: for the mouth of the LORD hath spoken it." (Isaiah 58:14)

As spiritual children of Israel by adoption through Jesus Christ, we have a great inheritance of prosperity. The road to victory won't be easy. However, you'll find that complaining is always easy—especially while you're travailing through the various wildernesses of life. However, I challenge you to find the good in every situation, standing on the promises of God. Even if that good is no more than the hope and prospect of a solution, such positive outlook is sure to activate you faith. And when your faith is activated, it moves the hand of God!

Hebrews 11:6 tells us that, "...without faith it is impossible to please him: for he that comes to God must believe that he is, and that he is a rewarder of them that diligently seek him."

God is looking for your faith. As He has already promised victory in Him, winning is only a matter of time. Therefore, from time to time, He allows the trials of life to mature us, taking us from faith to faith, preparing us for the battles ahead. And having received the instruction of His Word, He expects us to mix such with faith and apply it to our experiences: a divine recipe for success.

Having a positive attitude will take you a long way. The thoughts you think, the words you say, and your behavior in a given situation will have a powerful impact on your daily accomplishments. You will be comforted and motivated by that continual flow of positivity. Also, the people around you will be blessed—all because of your attitude. Moreover, a positive attitude with separate you from all those headed in the wrong direction, and ultimately it will win you favor with God against every Goliath in your path!

Joshua and Caleb were the only two men from their generation to enter into the Promised Land because of their faith—faith which was directly effected by a positive attitude and an obedient spirit.

***

So, as you prepare to enter into the Promised Land, activate your faith with these keys that you may be found pleasing in the sight of the Lord and energized to accomplish the task ahead.

Chapter 8: Forming Your Team

I've said it before, and I'll say it again: winning is never a solo act, it takes a team. What's more, by the same line of reasoning, one could also conclude that *losing* is also a team effort. And this would also be true.

For better or worse, the people around you have a profound effect on your life: they have a direct effect on whether or not you will win or lose—and *how* you when or lose.

In the story of Joseph, we saw that even though his brothers came against him, they were still a part of the team that propelled him into destiny, which eventually resulted in the prosperity of the children of Israel in Egypt. And in Numbers 13, we learned that even though the spies from the twelve tribes of Israel worked as a team to survey the land of Canaan, because they also came together in fear, they held an entire nation back from possessing the Promised Land.

With these things in mind, it is definitely clear that you should acknowledge the team that is all around you and the way that it is sure to affect your life. However, it is also clear that sometimes this team is not enough to render the kind of success that you desire—if it renders success at all. So, even after having *acknowledged* your team, you may still have to go ahead and *form* a team to achieve your goals.

So far, we've looked at the successes and failures of twelve brothers and twelve tribes: teams that were basically put together by the circumstances of life. Now let's look at the twelve disciples that were handpicked by our Lord and Savior Jesus Christ. Truly this was a dynamic team because it was comprised of individuals not simply *acknowledged*, but *appointed*.

Psalm 37:37 instructs us to, "Mark the perfect man, and behold the upright: for the end of that man is peace." Undoubtedly, Jesus was a perfect man and we can learn much from the decisions that He made in forming the team that would be His disciples, and ultimately the apostles of the Christian church. In this, we would be wise to copy His successful teamwork, forming our own teams to reflect the same composition that Jesus put together in selecting the disciples.

So, where do we begin?

To start, it should be noted that Jesus chose His disciples at the beginning of His ministry: twelve disciples, which, no doubt, mirrored the twelve tribes of Israel. From this we gather that a properly formed team should (preferably) be selected at the beginning of a project. It also helps if the team bears some symbolic significance, especially if your team is to address a particular audience that will be aware of its symbolism.

Jesus knew that his initial calling was to the Jews and that the Jews would likely recognize a round table of twelve Jewish men as a symbol of divine appointment. It's really that simple.

In terms of what this means for us: don't wait to the last minute to put your team together, and then don't just randomly put them together. The selection of your team should reflect good leadership in proper timing and careful planning with regard to the audience that you plan to meet.

During the Olympics, relay teams from all around the world are typically careful to select the correct number of team members needed to both qualify for the games and win the race. Moreover, each team member always bears his country's flag or colors. The team will usually train together for a great period of time—even if they train individually at first, they always come together at the right time, working toward the same goal, for the same country.

Unity is the key to successful teamwork. Each member of your team must have an understanding of the urgency at hand and a sense of the bigger picture. Each team member must have a vested interest in the success of the whole, understanding that, as a team player, his personal success is predicated on the success of the other team players that will help him cross the finish line. And Jesus understood this when He put the twelve disciples together.

However, more than unity in timing and symbolic significance, Jesus understood that His team needed to be flexible and diverse. Even though they were all Jews from the Middle East, the eclectic mix of personalities and backgrounds among the disciples served as the very foundation that Jesus would use to build a world enterprise that would literally reach every nation on earth.

Jesus knew that He needed to reach many different colors, creeds, cultures, and walks of life. The Gospel would be preached to *all* men—to *all* nations. Therefore, having a diverse team was essential to His plan. He didn't make the mistake of selecting people who were all the same. Though He was a perfect example, He didn't even expect His disciples to be exactly like Him in terms of personality and perspective. He preferred their personalities, opinions, and even their shortcomings, for He would use all of these things to form, train, and deploy a team that would radically change the world forever.

Everybody on your team doesn't have to be just like you. Yes, you may have the vision that will lead them all to victory. However, if your strategy is to clone yourself in order to win the race, you may find that when you stumble along the way, they'll stumble at the same time and in the same way—and just before the finish line.

Even if you think yourself to be near perfect, you are still capable of mistakes. Therefore, in forming your team, it would be wise to surround yourself with people that can counter your weaknesses and provide strength in balance. You will need people to perform different tasks and cover different areas. You need people that are good at different things and are able to approach a problem in different ways.

Now, if you find that you're already surrounded by a team like Joseph's contentious brothers or the cowardly spies of Israel, you'll definitely want to add a cupbearer or a Caleb to the mix. You need people that'll have your back and exhibit courage, especially if you're trying to break out of one of life's prisons or you're preparing to face some giants! You'll need a team like the one that Jesus put together.

That said, let's take a look at the twelve disciples…

Lists of the twelve disciples are found in each of the three Synoptic Gospels: Mark 3:13-19, Matthew 10:1-4, Luke 6:12-16. Of course, information about the disciples is also given in the Gospel of John, and throughout the New Testament.

We are first introduced to the twelve disciples in Mark:

> And He (Jesus) went up on the mountain and called to Him those He Himself wanted. And they came to Him. Then He appointed twelve, that they might be with Him and that He might send them out to preach, and to have power to heal sicknesses and to cast out demons: Simon, to whom He gave the name Peter; James the son of Zebedee and John the brother of James, to whom He gave the name Boanerges, that is, "Sons of Thunder"; Andrew, Philip, Bartholomew, Matthew, Thomas, James the son of Alphaeus, Thaddaeus, Simon the Cananite; and Judas Iscariot, who also betrayed Him. And they went into a house. (NKJV)

An analysis of each of the twelve disciples, based on information taken from the Bible, will reveal the qualities, characteristics, and the reasons behind Jesus' decision to select each of them in forming His team. Let's take a look at each one:

Peter

Simon, or Peter (as Jesus called him), is always the first disciple mentioned. This is because Peter was Jesus' right-hand man. A fisherman from Bethsaida of Galilee, Peter was given a leadership role among the disciples. Peter was chosen to be a cornerstone of the brotherhood and the ministry. In fact, Peter's named literally means "rock."

From the choice example of Peter, it should be obvious that you always want someone on your team who can handle things

Winning in Life

in case you're not there: someone that you trust, a right-hand man or *woman*.

The emphasis here is on capability and trust. The Peter on your team needs to both know the business and know you. And you need to know them to the point that you can be certain what their actions will be, especially in a problematic situation. This team member may be an old college buddy that shares your goals, or a spouse who's witnessed your journey and is prepared to go with you all the way. Selecting this team member is typically easy as they're usually one of those "acknowledged" team members already in place.

But sometimes you have to go out and find your Peter.

Jesus found Peter fishing, doing the very thing that He was going to commission him to do (symbolically speaking). Selecting a Peter means selecting someone of like mind and like spirit. No, this doesn't mean that they're exactly the same as you. But they will have the same goals—or, at the very least, the essential ability and interests necessary for the successful implementation of your project.

If you're looking to start a jazz trio, your Peter is probably going to be found at a jazz café. If you're that chef preparing to start a restaurant, you probably won't find your head manager at a sewage plant. If you're into business, your Peter *must* know the market. And while these things may seem obvious, you'd be surprised at how often people select the wrong person to appoint as the Peter of their team. Too often, they appoint Judas Iscariot instead (but we'll get to that later).

Now, Peter wasn't perfect. Anger and fear were two weaknesses that Peter had. Once, he displayed a violent streak when he cut off a man's ear in defense of Jesus in John 18:10 (noble, but not quite Jesus' method)—and another time he

Forming Your Team

denied Jesus thrice with cussing and swearing when the road got a little too rough and the going got a little too tough. (Read Matthew 26:69-74)

Yet, Jesus fully understood that all these acts were in the character of Peter, and He picked Peter nonetheless. When Jesus rose from the dead, He specifically instructed Mary to tell Peter of His resurrection. (Mark 16:7) Jesus knew that Peter was still the man for the job despite Peter's shortcomings, because Jesus knew Peter's heart.

In John 21:17 Jesus asked Peter three times, "Do you love me?" Peter earnestly answered, "Lord, you know all things; you know that I love you." Then Jesus replied, "Feed My sheep." Recall that in Mark 3, Jesus originally formed His team of disciples to, "send them out to preach, and to have power to heal sicknesses and to cast out demons." Jesus cared about people, and He commissioned Peter to care for others as well.

When Jesus asked his disciples, "Who do you say that I am?" in Matthew 16:15, Peter perceptively replied, "You are the Christ, the Son of the living God." Peter definitely understood who Jesus was, and respected the calling upon Jesus' life as the Son of God.

When selecting your Peter consider first the heart of the individual: their intent and perceptions. Do they care for the same things that you care for? Do they really know who you are and agree with your calling? If the answer to both of these questions is not "yes," then that's not your Peter.

Peter was an invaluable member of Jesus' team. And Jesus knew it. That's why He picked him. If you don't have a Peter on your team, it is essential that you go and find one. No winning team is complete without a "rock."

Andrew

Andrew was a fisherman by trade like his brother, Peter. He was also a former disciple of John the Baptist: a member of the movement that prepared the way for Jesus' arrival—and to such an extent that Andrew appropriately left John the Baptist and moved to follow Jesus upon His arrival. (John 1:35-40)

It is reasonable to believe that Andrew's being a disciple of John the Baptist prepared him to be a disciple of Christ. And he essentially began his discipleship by going to tell his brother Peter that he'd found the Messiah. (John 1:41)

Andrew had the combined experiences of being a fisherman and a student of the Word. He was the first of Jesus' disciples to recognize that Jesus was the Messiah and got excited about spreading the good news. Andrew had experience, insight, and initiative. In other words, he was a go-getter.

Every team needs members with experience, insight and initiative. The Andrews of your team are sure to grab hold of the vision and run with it. They bring to the table the skill sets necessary to kick things off to a great and energetic start. You'll always recognize an Andrew because you won't have to follow them around and make sure that they're doing their job. They're the kind of people that you can trust to just get the job done.

Get some Andrews on your team!

I can't emphasize this enough.

James and John: The Sons of Thunder

James and John were at the seashore with their father Zebedee when Jesus called them into discipleship—seemingly, out of the blue. And yet they came. Apparently, these men lived for such adventures. They had tremendous faith and were ones to heed the Word of the Lord.

John would write the Gospel of John and the Epistles of John, which showcase the divinity of Christ and His power to work in and through our lives. From the choice examples of James and John, we see the value in having people on your team that understand the importance of faith in God's Word.

It was John who said, "Now by this we know that we know Him, if we keep His commandments. He who says, 'I know Him,' and does not keep His commandments, is a liar, and the truth is not in him. But whoever keeps His *word*, truly the love of God is perfected in him. By this we know that we are in Him." (1 John 2: 3-5, NKJV)

James and John were of like spirit. They both understood that the Word of God is an anchor in the life of every Christian. He also declared that the will of God and the word of God are one and the same, "In the beginning was the Word, and the Word was with God, and the Word was God." (John 1:1)

You must have people on your team that understand the will of God as expounded in His Word. You need team members that know God's promises, as well as His method and strategies for winning in life.

Sometimes they may be a little "churchy," but that's okay. They'll always be on standby with an on-time word needed to encourage the team and offer some insight into what "thus sayeth the Lord." And this is always good to have because such will keep you from getting distracted by hype and gimmicks on the road to success. Such will keep you focused on your godly purpose.

People like James and John will keep you grounded in the Word of the Most High God. Their voices will ring loud and clear concerning trust and reverence in the Almighty. No wonder Jesus called them the "Sons of Thunder."

Find you a James and John.

Philip

Philip was also from Bethsaida of Galilee, like Andrew and Peter. He is most prominently featured in the Gospel of John.

On a certain occasion, some Greeks came to Philip asking to see Jesus. Though he had to inquire of Andrew first (probably to find out exactly where Jesus was or something along those lines), Philip promptly took the men to see the Master... (John 12:20–22)

Don't you just hate it when you have a problem at a department store and the customer service rep tells you, with an attitude, "I'm sorry, but there's nothing I can do." After all, isn't it their job to know what to do, or—at the very least—find someone else who can help?

It's been said before that, "You never get a second chance to make a first impression." And this saying is true. When it comes to problem solving and dealing with the public, you need someone on your team that knows how to deal with people. You need someone with "people skills." And someone who knows how to get answers that yield favorable results.

You need a Philip.

When those Greek men came to Philip, he was at their service. Yes, he went to Andrew first, for whatever reason. Still, he did accomplish the task of getting the men to Jesus. He found a way to help them.

Moreover, I imagine that there was something about Phillip that made the men comfortable approaching him. No doubt, he had an agreeable spirit and looked like he knew what was going on: like a disciple of Jesus Christ.

A Phillip will always represent you well. He'll be easy to work with, and typically look the part as to instill confidence in your audience. And that's what you need on your team: someone that people don't mind approaching for help or information, an agreeable liaison.

Depending on what your project is, this person may be a marketing guru, a press secretary, or a receptionist. Whatever capacity they serve in dealing with the public, having them on your team ensures a professional image, and a firm sense of organization. You'll never have to worry about missing an opportunity because someone walked away with the wrong impression of your team or you.

Simply put, a Philip will make you look good... and he'll do a lot of good for you.

Bartholomew, Thaddeus, and Simon the Zealot

Besides the listing of their names, the Bible doesn't say much about Bartholomew, Thaddeus, or Simon the Zealot. Apparently, these men worked behind the scenes. Nevertheless, they represent an essential component of teamwork.

You need behind-the-scenes workers. You need people on your team that are willing to work away from the spotlight. You need people that are fine with performing small but significant tasks. These kinds of people are never out front on the big screen but have their names rolling in the end credits nonetheless: the personal assistant, the hairdresser, the security guard, or the coffee man.

A Bartholomew will never complain that he's not being recognized. Though he may be well-deserving of recognition, a Thaddeus will rarely ask for a raise as a condition of his faithful service. A Simon will always remain zealous, taking pride in his work even when no one's around to see it besides him.

Now, this doesn't mean that you should take them for granted. In fact, you should show your appreciation for them all the more affirming their importance as members of the team.

Without the behind-the-scenes players most of the simple tasks will never get done. Consequently, those assigned bigger tasks will become distracted by things that they shouldn't even have to worry about. Without the behind-the-scenes players the entire team effort is liable to collapse under a weight of frustration and disorganization.

Thank God for Bartholomew, Thaddeus, and Simon! Make sure that they're recognized. If you can afford it, give them a raise. And always share in the zeal of their efforts, especially those that most people will never see besides them. They bring so much to the table. Perhaps more than words can express.

Matthew

The Roman era in which Jesus and the disciples lived wasn't much different from our own in at least one respect: taxes. In much the same way as today, people didn't like tax collectors back then. However, this didn't stop Jesus from commissioning such a man to be a part of His team.

Matthew was a tax collector.

Not only was Matthew good at handling money, he was also good at handling people when it came to getting money owed. And whatever you may think of Matthew's profession, the bottom line is this: you need someone on your team who can take care of business and manage the cash flow.

Money is a part of life. Resources are necessary for the upbuilding of God's kingdom. If you and your team are not good stewards over your finances, your efforts toward financial prosperity are sure to fail. Even though it is God's desire that you would prosper, it is up to you to make the most of what He has given you to accomplish that task. And this includes making sure that you have people on your team that know how to manage your prosperity: businessmen, bookkeepers, trustees, and even bill collectors.

Matthew also wrote the Gospel of Matthew. From this we can gather that Matthew was witness to the majesty of Christ in prosperity of various sorts: financial, health, and spiritual. In other words, for Matthew, even though he could handle the money, it wasn't about the millions. It was about purpose. Matthew understood what Jesus came to earth to do, and he determined in his heart to go with Jesus all the way.

When selecting the people that are going to handle your money, be careful not to select those who just want to be around money. Rather, select those who want to be around *you* because they believe in the purpose and calling that God has on your life. Select trustworthy people that want to see you prosper, and you can be sure that they will handle your prosperity and the people connected to it in the right way.

Select a Matthew.

Thomas

Often times he is referred to as "Doubting Thomas" because he didn't believe that Jesus had risen from the dead when the other disciples told him about it. (John 20:19-28)

The other disciples had already seen the resurrected Christ, but Thomas had yet to see anyone rise from the dead. Therefore, having witnessed Jesus' brutal and devastating crucifixion, any man would be hard pressed to believe that one could come back from such, unless the resurrected one was standing before him. Thomas was simply guilty of wanting to experience the same thing that the other disciples had experienced.

Thomas' mistake was not that he did not believe the other disciples, but that he doubted what Jesus had said before the crucifixion: that Christ would rise after three days.

Granted, Thomas was from the "show me" state. And that's probably why Jesus chose him.

Yes, faith is important. But faith in Jesus' presence is not the same as "blind faith" in someone else's testimony—no matter whose testimony it is. Some things you just need to see for yourself.

Therefore, it is often necessary to have someone on your team that will not be satisfied with hearsay, but prefers to get a literal confirmation of God's promises—to get a *visual*, and behold the manifestation of His miracle-working power firsthand.

A Thomas will never be satisfied that someone got healed at *last year's* revival. A Thomas will never be impressed that the company used to turn a profit. A Thomas will never be content in the successes of yesteryear. Rather, he will always look to see what God is doing today. And even if everybody else agrees that someone's testimony truly declares a manifestation of God, a Thomas will choose to experience it himself before drawing his conclusion.

Having a Thomas on your team provides a valuable perspective. Jesus had no problem proving himself to Thomas because He understood that sometimes an increase of faith simply requires an increase of manifestation. No doubt, this experience of manifestation strengthened Thomas' faith and helped him to overcome future challenges in life.

Don't despise the Thomas on your team. Instead, pray that God would reveal Himself, taking that Thomas from faith to faith—and everyone else to the next level as well.

James, son of Alphaeus

Now, James was a man of faith. He wrote the book of James, which describes the dynamic power of faith that can be demonstrated through our works and by our deeds. It was James who said, "…faith without works is dead." (James 2:26) James understood that believing in a vision means more than just talk. It means working hard to see that it is accomplished.

When forming your team, pick people that are willing to back up their words with action. Pick people that are willing to step out of their comfort zones, by faith, to be a part of something that is bigger than them.

Don't forget, you need a James.

Judas Iscariot

Contrary to what many theologians may believe, Jesus did not pick Judas to betray him. Like any masterful teacher, Jesus desired to train Judas in the way of godliness despite his shortcomings, giving him a fair opportunity to reach his full potential as a member of the team.

Apparently, Jesus saw something of value in Judas.

Granted, Jesus did not make Judas his right-hand man. Still, Jesus did entrust him with a certain level of responsibility, for Judas was allowed to carry the disciple's "money bag." (John 13:29) Unfortunately, Judas became too fixated on money, and this was ultimately his undoing.

Judas could have been an Apostle. However, he chose to betray Jesus for 30 pieces of silver: a costly mistake. One mistake cost him his peace of mind, his place in the kingdom of God, and ultimately it cost him his life. Even though Judas was devastated after his decision and tried to give the money back, it was too late to change what had been done. (Matthew 27:3) And so Judas committed suicide—another mistake.

Who's to say that Jesus would not have forgiven Judas? He forgave Peter, didn't He?

Have you ever known someone who perhaps started off meaning well but was prone to making a series of bad decisions? It should be obvious that these kinds of people bear watching. Though, most of the time, we won't pick a Judas to be on our team outright. However, too often an acknowledged member of the team with a certain potential turns out to be a Judas.

Even though he is given an opportunity to better himself and experience the favor of God operating in his life, a Judas will decide to just hold on to the "money bag": that thing that he sees as being more valuable initially. For example, a Judas might attempt to ruin your reputation to better his own. A Judas might be jealous of your anointing and scandalize your name, and never attempt to apologize until after you've been "crucified" by those who once loved you, respected you, or at least admired what you stood for.

You'll also recall Matthew 26:48, "Now the betrayer had given them a sign, saying, 'The one I shall kiss is the man; seize him.' And he came up to Jesus at once and said, 'Hail Master!' And he kissed him."

A Judas is usually a kiss-up. Unfortunately, the warmest greeting from the "most supportive" doesn't always come with best wishes or the right intent.

So what should you do if you find a Judas on your team?

Try to approach your Judas situation the way Jesus did. Jesus understood that Judas was not the devil. The *devil* is the devil. Sadly, Judas allowed the devil to influence his decision making. All the while Jesus was fully aware of what was going on. So, it didn't take Him by surprise when Judas did what he did. In this, we see that you should always have your eyes and ears open, employing a spirit of discernment when dealing with each team member. And never hesitate to do as Jesus did. Jesus said to him, "Friend why are you here?" (Matthew 26:50) In other words, "What's up with this?"

Now, keep in mind that, most of the time, people mean well. But this doesn't render them immune to temptation and making horrible mistakes. Don't just go flying off the cuff, however, calling people "Judas!" every time they make a mistake. Do as Jesus did and deal with the situation responsibly, remembering why you chose that person to be on your team in the first place. Maybe they will fix the situation or in some other way choose to do the right thing. And if it becomes certain that they won't, let them move on.

Finally, I will say that it was God's will that Jesus should die on the cross for our sins. If Judas had not betrayed Jesus, Jesus would have still gone to the cross by some other series of events. Know that your future is in the hands of God. Judas or no Judas, nothing can hold you back from fulfilling your destiny in Him!

***

As you can see Jesus had a very dynamic team in the twelve disciples because He chose to cover every area necessary for success. And you should form your team likewise: a right-hand man like Peter; a go-getter like Andrew; men of the Word like James and John: the Sons of Thunder; a people person like Philip; people to work behind the scenes like Bartholomew, Thaddeus, and Simon; someone who knows finance like Matthew; someone from the "show me" state like Thomas; a man of faith like James; and sometimes even an x-factor with a certain potential like Judas.

Make sure you select team members that will work well together. And once you've selected your team, *let* your team be your team. When Jesus sent the disciples out in pairs to accomplish the goals of ministry, He wasn't there for every moment of the day looking over their shoulders to make sure that they were casting out demons or healing the sick.

Once you've put in the proper research and discernment to select the best you can find, that's it. Trust the decisions that you've made and the people that you've put in place. In other words, get out of the way and let your team work for you. After all, isn't that why you formed a team in the first place?

From time to time you may have to make adjustments. Often, change is necessary to ensure and maintain success. You may have to let Judas go, forgive Peter, and give Thaddaeus a raise. Such is simply a part of the leadership process, and the process for winning in life. In all these things, you'll be glad to have a dynamic team to help you win the race.

Forming your team is one of the most significant choices that you'll ever make. Do so wisely.

Chapter 9: Move into Action

Okay, at this point you've prepared yourself and your team to succeed. You've learned that a team's success can be measured by the individual successes of its members; you've discovered who you are and the calling upon your life; with the winner's attitude, you've set realistic goals and acknowledged the various factors that lead to success; you've set strategies for winning, activating your faith and forming the right team to help you meet the challenges ahead. There's only one thing left for you to do...

Move into action!

After you've done all the work necessary to prepare yourself for success, the only thing left to do is to go out and succeed. No matter how much you've trained for the race, you can't win the race if you don't run. No matter how much you stretch the bow with the arrow in place, it will never nail the target if you don't let it go. Even after you've overcome your fear of giants,

Moving Into Action

you will still have to face them if you intend to inherit the Promised Land.

Action is the most determinate factor when it comes to winning in life. What you do determines what you have. Without a doubt, moving into action is the only way to reach your destiny.

Note: a good move is always preceded by preparation. It's not a "spur of the moment" kind of thing. A good move must take into account your history and goals. This also includes an understanding of the obstacles that you will face. And all this will be culminated in a single moment—the very moment that you *physically* step out.

The generation of Israel that was delivered from Egypt was not the same generation that inherited the Promised Land. Unfortunately, the entire nation's destiny was delayed because one generation refused to move into action for reasons of fear.

Despite an awesome history with the God of Abraham, Isaac and Jacob, Israel did not believe in what God had deposited into them to defeat the giant inhabitants of the land of Canaan. Consequently, they did not move into action. Apparently, they were more *comfortable* hanging out at the gates complaining about the situation. Consequently, they allowed their "comfort zone" to become a prison: a 40 year life sentence in the wilderness.

"Comfort zones" are famous for—well, being *comfortable*. They represent a place in life where you feel that you have a certain level of control. And whereas they may not be comfortable in the sense that they provide everything that you want, it is easy enough to find contentment in them because, at the very least, they allow you to avoid what you don't want… or so it would seem.

The truth of the matter is that comfort zones can be very dangerous. We often settle into a comfort zone trying to avoid failure. However, as time goes on, we discover that a comfort zone can ironically be the very seat of failure. At first, your comfort zone allows you a place to formulate your dreams. But in the end, it locks you in and you end up not living your dreams at all. The reason for this is because comfort zones are designated to inhibit change in an ever-changing world. In this, they are not flexible, and typically don't allow you to change.

People in their comfort zones will look at the way things have always been done, and conclude that such is the way things should always be done. They will stubbornly look to the past to determine what is best for the future. Consequently, the issues of the present usually end up getting stuck somewhere in between.

If you've never stood up for yourself in the past and you're use to this, what's the chance of you actually challenging Goliath? If you're certain that you'll fail in an area where you desire to win, even though you may want to succeed, how much more likely are you to say, "Well, maybe it's just not for me"? If you're convinced that something will surely happen *one day*, how motivated will you be to make it happen *today*?

Have you ever made a New Year's resolution?

Usually such resolutions reflect a myriad of dreams and goals that did not come into fruition during the previous year or *years*. Many times we are comfortable with setting goals and even doing a little preparatory work. However, when it comes to actually making them happen, something about the situations of life cause us to remain content in our comfort zones: the comfort zone of old habits or the same old excuses.

Yes, stepping out of your comfort zone can be hard to do, especially if you're waiting for that moment when everything will be "just perfect": "I'll pursue my dream once the kids finish school"; "I'll go on a diet and lose weight after the holidays"; "I'll start saving money after the Lord blesses my finances."

Excuse after excuse, comfort zones can hold you back. The "perfect moment" may never come. So, snap out of it! Stop holding yourself back. At some point, you will have to make up in your mind that you're just going to move out into action. You'll have to step out on faith, just like Abraham did.

Abraham is often called the "Father of Faith." Time after time throughout the Bible, Abraham had to step out of his comfort zone and into the realm of *living* faith. He had to move into action to see the promises of God fulfilled in his life.

Abraham's story begins in Genesis 12:

Now the LORD had said to Abram:

> "Get out of your country,
> From your family
> And from your father's house,
> To a land that I will show you.
>
> I will make you a great nation;
> I will bless you
> And make your name great;
> And you shall be a blessing.
>
> I will bless those who bless you,
> And I will curse him who curses you;
> And in you all the families of the earth shall be blessed."

Winning in Life

So Abram departed as the LORD had spoken to him, and Lot went with him. And Abram was seventy-five years old when he departed from Haran. Then Abram took Sarai his wife and Lot his brother's son, and all their possessions that they had gathered, and the people whom they had acquired in Haran, and they departed to go to the land of Canaan. So they came to the land of Canaan. Abram passed through the land to the place of Shechem, as far as the terebinth tree of Moreh. And the Canaanites were then in the land.

Then the LORD appeared to Abram and said, "To your descendants I will give this land." And there he built an altar to the LORD, who had appeared to him… (NKJV)

***

Originally, Abraham's name was "Abram," which means "high father" in Hebrew. This name bore great prophetic significance as it foreshadowed Abraham's destiny to become a highly respected patriarch. However, in Genesis 17:5, God took it up a level and renamed Abram "Abraham," which means "father of many." God promised Abraham that he would be the father of many, and that his descendents would inherit the land of Canaan—the very land that God had shown him.

But before he even saw the land, Abraham had to move out of his comfort zone, away from his father's house in Haran. Even though Abraham probably had some inheritance back home, he chose to pursue a greater blessing based on the Word of God. He heard the voice of the Lord, took his wife and his nephew (members of his team), and then moved out!

From the example of Abraham, we can learn a few things about moving into action.

First, Abraham was not a procrastinator. As soon as he heard the word of the Lord, he moved out. At 75 years old, time was of the essence. Undoubtedly, the calling to become a "father of many nations" was a time-sensitive project. After all, Abraham and his wife had no children when he received the Word, and they weren't getting any younger.

Have you ever felt like you had all the time in the world to make something happen? Or, in the more likely scenario, you knew that there was a definite deadline, but, for whatever reason you decided to put your work off. Did you dread the work ahead? Or maybe you just didn't have a sense of urgency and felt that other things should take priority.

When it comes to the way that you use your time and the way that you live your life, nothing is more important than walking in your calling and meeting your destiny. Period.

God desires for you to live a full and meaningful life: a life of purpose—and not just any purpose, but *your* purpose. There is something that you're meant to do on this earth, and the activities of your journey should reflect an understanding and a *reaching* toward this goal.

Maybe you are called to be a good parent. Perhaps you are destined to be the president of the United States. Are you the musician, the chef, or the businessman? Maybe you're a pastor or the doctor who shall discover a cure for cancer or AIDS.

Whatever it is that you are meant to be, the world around you is counting on you to be in place and to do that thing that you do best. You don't have time to procrastinate.

Now, this is not to say that you should be in a rush to fulfill your destiny. However, you certainly shouldn't be distracted by a bunch of things that have nothing to do with your calling. As soon as you discover that thing that is meant for you to do, you should be occupied doing it. By the power and grace of God, you should be meeting goals. You should be living the life to which you are called. Any other life would be pointless.

So, from the example of Abraham, we see that timing is important. It is important to move out as soon as the Lord speaks. And God speaks in a variety of ways. He speaks through people and the circumstances of life. He speaks through His Word—and He may be trying to speak through you!

Many times, moving into action will require that you be a mouthpiece, especially if you're the leader of your team—or even if you just have a responsibility to the team.

Abraham's team (his wife Sarai, his nephew Lot, and the people whom they had acquired in Haran) moved out based on his word. In this, we see that Abraham was a leader with initiative. And the "leader's initiative" is required for moving into action, whether you're leading just yourself or many.

Having the leader's initiative is all about making timely and decisive choices. Perhaps the greatest choice that you'll ever have to make as a leader is the choice to move out, especially under adverse or inconvenient circumstances.

Sometimes you'll have to motivate yourself to "just do it." You'll have to do like David did and encourage yourself in the Lord. (1 Samuel 30:6) Also, there are times you'll have to encourage others and lead them into uncharted territory. Whereas the whole team may be hesitant, sometimes your initiative in giving the word to "go ahead" is all that's needed to boost confidence and send the team off on the road to victory.

Though you may be unsure of what the future holds, after you've prepared to move out, the only thing left to do is to be courageous and move out—even in the midst of some uncertainty or in the face of giants and fortified cities...

When the children of Israel finally moved into action and began their conquest of the land of Canaan at the Battle of Jericho, they were under the leadership of Joshua (Moses' right-hand man). Ironically, by this time Moses was no longer with them. And there is a valuable lesson to be learned in the reason why Moses was not allowed to cross over Jordan.

As you move out it is important to move out in the way that God has instructed you to. Moses did not go into the Promised Land because, on a certain occasion, he did not deal with the children of Israel in the manner that God had instructed him to. Let's take a look at the story...

Numbers 20

Then the children of Israel, the whole congregation, came into the Wilderness of Zin in the first month, and the people stayed in Kadesh; and Miriam died there and was buried there.

Now there was no water for the congregation; so they gathered together against Moses and Aaron. And the people contended with Moses and spoke, saying: "If only we had died when our brethren died before the LORD! Why have you brought up the assembly of the LORD into this wilderness, that we and our animals should die here? And why have you made us come up out of Egypt, to bring us to this evil place? It is not a place of grain or figs or vines or pomegranates; nor is there any water to drink." So Moses and Aaron went from the presence of the assembly to the door of the tabernacle of meeting, and they fell on their faces. And the glory of the LORD appeared to them.

Then the LORD spoke to Moses, saying, "Take the rod; you and your brother Aaron gather the congregation together. Speak to the rock before their eyes, and it will yield its water; thus you shall bring water for them out of the rock, and give drink to the congregation and their animals." So Moses took the rod from before the LORD as He commanded him.

And Moses and Aaron gathered the assembly together before the rock; and he said to them, "Hear now, you rebels! Must we bring water for you out of this rock?" Then Moses lifted his hand and struck the rock twice with his rod; and water came out abundantly, and the congregation and their animals drank.

Then the LORD spoke to Moses and Aaron, "Because you did not believe Me, to hallow Me in the eyes of the children of Israel, therefore you shall not bring this assembly into the land which I have given them."

This was the water of Meribah, because the children of Israel contended with the LORD, and He was hallowed among them. (NKJV)

***

Much like everything else when it comes to winning, moving out is a process. Moreover, it is a process that requires obedience: you can't just move out any ol' kind of way. Remember, God has a plan for our lives. When we forsake or challenge the integrity of God's guidance, we hold ourselves back—and in the worst case scenario, we totally miss out.

God told Moses to speak to the stone, but Moses decided to strike it instead. As a leader, he had become frustrated with his team (the children of Israel). This, in turn, caused him to step out of his calling as one guided by the Word of the Lord. A single act of disobedience was enough to alter his destiny.

Yes, your destiny can be altered significantly when you step outside of the will of God. While your future is not written in stone, your ultimate success may be contingent on whether you speak to the stone or strike it instead. In other words, your future is based on the choices that you make and can only truly be benefited by you making choices that reflect the perfect will of God, following His instructions.

And don't think you've gotten away just because water still comes out of the rock after you've *struck* it. If God told you to *speak* to it, that's precisely what He meant. Remember there will be consequences for disobedience.

The place where the water was given to the children of Israel from the rock was called Meribah, which means "abundance." Many times when God has brought you and your team to a place of predestinated abundance, He will be gracious enough to bless you despite your shortcomings that He may be "hallowed" among the people—that is *glorified*. However, rest assured that God keeps an account of your actions. It is as Galatians 6:7 says, "Be not deceived; God is not mocked: for whatsoever a man sows, that shall he also reap."

There's a right way to do things. God has provided us instructions in His word to teach us this way. It is up to you to follow these instructions and not allow anyone or anything to steer you off course—especially not the members of your team, be they family, friends, or enemies.

Remember that "I" in team? No matter who's on your team, as the leader of your team, you are ultimately responsible for meeting your destiny. Yes, you will have to deal with people as they are an essential part of the journey. However, keep in mind that it's important that *you* cross the finish line. As God has given you everything necessary for success, if you don't cross the finish line you won't be able to blame anyone but yourself.

Therefore, run the course in the way that God has laid it out, letting His word be the "lamp unto your feet, and the light unto your path." (Psalm 119:105) Be mindful of what you've set out to do and where your help comes from. Your help comes from the Lord. So, learn to work with *yourself* and your team to accomplish your goals in the right way—that is, God's way.

When God led the children of Israel over the river of Jordan to the city of Jericho, He gave Joshua specific instructions about how to conquer the city. Let's take a look...

Joshua 6

Now Jericho was securely shut up because of the children of Israel; none went out, and none came in. And the LORD said to Joshua: "See! I have given Jericho into your hand, its king, and the mighty men of valor. You shall march around the city, all you men of war; you shall go all around the city once. This you shall do six days. And seven priests shall bear seven trumpets of rams' horns before the ark. But the seventh day you shall march around the city seven times, and the priests shall blow the trumpets. It shall come to pass, when they make a long blast with the ram's horn, and when you hear the sound of the trumpet, that all the people shall shout with a great shout; then the wall of the city will fall down flat. And the people shall go up every man straight before him."

Then Joshua the son of Nun called the priests and said to them, "Take up the ark of the covenant, and let seven priests bear seven trumpets of rams' horns before the ark of the LORD." And he said to the people, "Proceed, and march

Moving Into Action

around the city, and let him who is armed advance before the ark of the LORD."

So it was, when Joshua had spoken to the people, that the seven priests bearing the seven trumpets of rams' horns before the LORD advanced and blew the trumpets, and the ark of the covenant of the LORD followed them. The armed men went before the priests who blew the trumpets, and the rear guard came after the ark, while the priests continued blowing the trumpets.

Now Joshua had commanded the people, saying, "You shall not shout or make any noise with your voice, nor shall a word proceed out of your mouth, until the day I say to you, 'Shout!' Then you shall shout." So he had the ark of the LORD circle the city, going around it once. Then they came into the camp and lodged in the camp.

And Joshua rose early in the morning, and the priests took up the ark of the LORD. Then seven priests bearing seven trumpets of rams' horns before the ark of the LORD went on continually and blew with the trumpets. And the armed men went before them. But the rear guard came after the ark of the LORD, while the priests continued blowing the trumpets. And the second day they marched around the city once and returned to the camp. So they did six days.

But it came to pass on the seventh day that they rose early, about the dawning of the day, and marched around the city seven times in the same manner. On that day only they marched around the city seven times. And the seventh time it happened, when the priests blew the trumpets, that Joshua said to the people: "Shout, for the LORD has given you the city! Now the city shall be doomed by the LORD to destruction, it and all who are in it. Only Rahab the harlot shall live, she and all who are with her in the house, because she hid the messengers that we sent. And you, by all means abstain from the accursed things, lest you become accursed when you take of the accursed things, and make the camp of Israel a curse, and trouble it. But all the silver and gold, and vessels of bronze and iron, are consecrated to the LORD; they shall come into the treasury of the LORD."

So the people shouted when the priests blew the trumpets. And it happened when the people heard the sound of the trumpet, and the people shouted with a great shout, that the wall fell down flat. Then the people went up into the city, every man straight before him, and they took the city. (NKJV)

***

God instructed Joshua to have the children of Israel march around the city of Jericho for six days—in silence! The priests were to carry the "ark of the Lord" and everyone was to refrain from making any noise, until they were commanded to blow the trumpets and shout on the seventh day.

In Biblical numerology, the number seven represents the number of completion. The ark of the Lord (also known as the Ark of the Covenant) literally represented the presence of God and the agreement that He had with His people: that they would reverence Him, and that He would, in turn, prosper them.

In all these things, we can gather that moving into action may require a period of *resting* in the Lord, which was symbolized in Israel's silence. This includes refraining from complaints, words of negativity, expressions of doubt—or any such *noise*. Then, after the timing and preparation necessary for the success is complete, symbolically represented by Israel marching for seven days, decisive action is required—a shout!

Moving Into Action

Victors commonly shout upon momentous victories. You've probably seen such at the Olympics when the winning team receives the coveted gold. Shouting declares decisive victory, and that which is a direct result of decisive action.

Are you ready to shout? If so, move into action!

The walls of Jericho fell because Israel moved into action, following God's instructions. And as a result of Joshua's obedience, Israel took the city and the fame of their conquest spread throughout the entire land of Canaan. (Joshua 6:27) No doubt, word got back to the giants and all of the other opponents that they would eventually face and defeat.

Israel won because they did it the Lord's way—with emphasis on the fact that they *did* it. With God on your team, victory is inevitable. But this victory requires that you move into action, and that you do it the right way. After you've done all the work necessary to succeed, don't forget the last and most important step. Don't procrastinate. Move out of your comfort zone, stretch the bow and release the arrow! It's time to meet your destiny at the finish line.

Move into action!

Chapter 10:
3 Keys to Maintaining Victory

So, you did what you needed to do, moved into action, and now you're winning. Oh, the sweet taste of victory—but wait, your journey doesn't necessarily end here. Even after you've become victorious, there is yet more to be done: you still need to *maintain* the victory.

We've all heard stories about superior athletes who remained undefeated during their prime. However, as time went on, various situations and circumstances took them off their game and they ended up being defeated by the new kid on the block. Nothing is more devastating than having the victory and then losing it. Wouldn't you agree? Therefore, maintaining the victory is the key to living a successful *lifestyle*.

Like everything else when it comes to winning, maintenance is also a process. The following *3 Keys to Maintaining Victory* will help you complete the process and remain victorious. With these keys you will enjoy winning in life for many years to come.

Key #1: Integrity

Whatever it took to gain the victory will also be what it will take to maintain the victory: you must be consistent...

Integrity is signified by a state of *consistency* in terms of character, quality of performance, and successful methods of operation.

A successful musician must continue to play his instrument throughout his entire lifetime in order to remain the best at what he does. Even if the masterful chef starts a chain of restaurants with many qualified chefs and managers that report to him on a regular basis, every now and again you'll still find him in the kitchen cooking up that special recipe, as no one else can. And the multi-billionaire businessman will always keep up with the markets, and leave his yacht once in a while to visit the office and make sure everything is running smoothly—that is, if he desires to remain on top.

Remaining integral basically means that you don't allow the good things about yourself and your ways to change with time or circumstance. It has everything to do with identifying what works well and never falling below this standard. The respect that you receive from colleagues and others in your field is typically based on some reputation of integrity. People will remember how you've successfully operated in the past, and they'll expect you to bring your A-game every time.

Half of your victory will be based on the effort of your team. In this, you should always seek to preserve the integrity of your team. In other words, don't get rid of the people that helped you reach the top. And while this may seem obvious, you would be surprised at how many operations started off winning because of the right team, but eventually fell back—or failed completely—because somebody thought that the project would remain successful without its key players.

Don't forsake a good and faithful team member just because someone else comes along with a fancier resume or runs in a more "sophisticated" circle. Moreover, don't let certain fall-outs cause you to lose sight of someone's value. Even though Peter denied Jesus at the worst possible time, Jesus forgave Peter and held on to him because He understood Peter's value to the team, and that he could not be easily replaced.

Before you decide to demote someone, or get caught up in the notion that they're replaceable, remember their contribution to your success and ask yourself, "Could I have done it without them?"—or more importantly, "*Did* I do it without them?"

In preparation for his victory at the battle of Jericho, Joshua sent spies into the walled city. The spies were assisted by a prostitute named Rahab. On that day when the walls were brought down, Joshua commanded Israel with these words, "Shout! For the LORD has given you the city! The city and all that is in it are to be devoted to the LORD. Only Rahab the prostitute and all who are with her in her house shall be spared, because she hid the spies we sent." (Joshua 6:17)

Although she was not of the children of Israel, Joshua remembered Rahab and honored her as a member of his team. He didn't think any less of her contribution because of her "occupation." He kept her on the team and eventually Rahab married into the nation of Israel and became the great-great grandmother of King David! And as you know, Jesus was the son of David! (See Matthew 1:5)

If you needed a Rahab to hide the "spies" (that is, protect your interests), there's a good chance that you will need a Rahab's assistance somewhere down the road. By keeping a Rahab's essential qualities in mind, you won't soon forget the numerous sacrifices—and often the risks that a Rahab takes in order to see you come out successfully on top. So, at all cost, preserve the integrity of your team, valuing their individual contributions and respecting their positions.

Now, this is not to say that you'll never have to change the composition of your team, whether this means demoting someone or taking them out all together. The point is simply this: know the value of who you have and keep them on for as long as they are of value.

The other half of your victory is based on who you are. You will find that integrity is best maintained when you are walking in your divine calling. For this is what allowed you to be placed on the path of success, with a guaranteed opportunity to win in life.

Sometimes great success can lure us into believing that we are winning because of something other than the original means of victory. Just because you're tremendously successful in one area doesn't mean that you should go off and try your hand at something else just because it's a "good idea" or because everyone says that you would be good at it. Never forget what you're *really* good at, and what you're meant to do. When you're winning the race, resist all temptation to move outside of your lane.

Remaining integral requires holding on to the best of who you are. Don't allow success to change you in a negative way. If you were down-to-earth when you started off, stay down-to-earth. Maintain a certain level of accessibility and open-mindedness, and remember that humility is among the noblest qualities of good leadership. Hold on to the things that your audience loves about you, and you will be sure to continue your success in dealing with them for many, many years to come.

Key #2: Innovation

Yes, integrity is all about being consistent in the good things. However, as you hold on to the good things, always remain open to the idea that there may be something *better*.

Every day new problems arise that require new solutions. The challenges of tomorrow may not be met by the strategies of yesterday. We live in an ever-changing world and it is imperative that you learn to flow and change with it as is necessary to maintain your status as a winner. Don't allow your success to become a dreaded comfort zone where new and exciting victories become a thing of the past. Rather, keep an open mind and gladly receive every opportunity to think outside of the box.

And you'll know when it's time to move to the next level when you discover that the seat of your success is no longer suited to be at the table of your ambitions. In that moment, the luster of your past victories will begin to fade. Moreover, like that star athlete, you might find yourself preparing to face the new kid on the block. When that time comes, staying on top may require a new approach. In order to maintain victory, you'll have to embrace the *spirit of innovation*.

The spirit of innovation seeks to improve upon solutions that have already been found and to find solutions for problems that are likely to surface. Being innovative means investing in your winning edge: fine-tuning your methods, improving your strategies, and asking yourself the brave questions today that will lead to the breakthrough answers of tomorrow:

Is there a better way to do *this*?

What would we do if *that* happened?

Yes, that *was* the trend then, but what is the trend *now*?

There can be great value in having an established way of doing things. The "old way" has its place and it should be respected and appreciated for its contribution to your success. However, unless you plan on remaining "old" and falling behind the times, at some point you're going to have to embrace the new.

The presence of newness signifies life and progress. It is a must have for every advancing team. And when it comes to integrating the new, Jesus gave this advice, "...no one puts new wine into old wineskins; or else the new wine bursts the wineskins, the wine is spilled, and the wineskins are ruined. But new wine must be put into new wineskins." (Mark 2:22)

Never try to force the new way to conform to the old way. Yes, the new way should meet and even exceed the same goals and standards as the old. But understand that the new way may not accomplish success by the same methods or means. Many times trying to force the old into the new (and vice versa) will only result in casualty on both sides.

A smooth and successful transition from the old to the new will require a patient and appropriate introduction of the new, while respecting what works about the old. In this, don't just choose something new just because it's new. If the new doesn't improve upon the old, it may be better to keep the old until a more worthy strategy or solution can be found.

At the same time, in the spirit of progress, you should be exploring new ideas and giving them a chance to work. Often the new way will require some getting use to. Granted, this can be difficult at times—especially if you're use to maintaining a certain perspective and seeing things done a certain way. However, embracing the new way often requires a new way of thinking.

The musician may have successfully worked with his jazz trio for years. But the time may come when he wants to start a big band. He shouldn't necessarily force the old players to play in the new band, but he may still want to incorporate some of the old repertoire of jazz standards, using what works and just giving it a bigger sound. That's innovation.

The master chef might be presented with a new recipe. Granted, it will have to past the test of his taste buds before he chooses to add it to the menu. Still, if he really wants to give it a try, he shouldn't keep adding his own herbs and spices until it taste just like another dish that he has prepared time and again. For what would be the progress in that?

And the multi-billionaire businessman may have to hire a new CEO with fresh ideas. Even so, that new guy shouldn't be expected to think or operate like the old guy. By the same token, the new guy shouldn't expect everyone in the firm to warm up to him overnight. The transition will definitely take time and patience.

Patience is the water that nurtures a seed of innovation. It is definitely necessary. Often a sprouting seed of innovation must break ground of monumental proportions; rightly so, the new is expected to succeed where the old way may have failed or is likely to eventually fail. In this, innovation is not only about finding a solution to a particular problem, but also about finding a problem before it finds you.

Sometimes the comforts of the Promised Land will cause us to forget that there are still Goliaths out there. Maintaining victory is about fixing problems before they even surface, just as much as it is about addressing issues that have already surfaced. Don't make the mistake of letting your guard down. You should always be looking for dynamic ways to meet ever-present challenges and the inevitable battles ahead.

So, go ahead. Be innovative. Find a challenge; find a solution. Find something that needs to be fixed and fix it. There will always be some area of your operation that could use improvement. Such is the place where the spirit of innovation resides and is the path to maintaining victory.

Key #3: Inspection

The mark of mastery is in the details. To maintain the victory you must continually *inspect* the work that you and your team put out. Quality control is of the utmost importance.

Inspection goes behind integrity and innovation. Whereas integrity seeks to maintain the good, and innovation seeks to improve upon that, inspection journeys beneath the surface of our successes and failures and gets down to the nitty-gritty. Inspection is the tool used to make sure that integrity remains sound and that innovations are resourceful.

Yes, everything may be fine on the surface. You may have a good reputation among your constituents and ingenious breakthroughs may be on the horizon. However, if you do not inspect your work all these things may fall victim to an unsightly oversight. Your Promised Land will undoubtedly be abundant with giant clusters of grapes that you plan to enjoy. Though beware: many times it is the small foxes that destroy the vine. (Song of Solomon 2:15)

Winning in Life

Always be aware of and on the look out for the little things that may be eroding your success, things that could have easily been fixed—had they not gone unchecked: maybe a customer service rep had a bad attitude one day and nobody but the customers noticed; maybe the restrooms aren't the cleanest and that's why fewer and fewer customers are coming to your restaurant; maybe you're spending just 2¢ too much on each of the 1 million advertisements that you sent out, a $20,000 consequence.

Little problems have a tendency to get pretty big in a short period of time. The most effective resource that you'll have to combat such devastation is a consistent inspection of every aspect of what you and your team does.

Inspection has a lot to do with training. It is important to make sure that all members of the team are on the same page, that they share the same vision, and that they speak the same message in situations wherein they represent the team. You definitely don't want your team to behave one way during training, and then another way on the field. Away missions are especially crucial. Proper inspections of your team may require that you meet them in the boardroom as well as the boardinghouse.

Now, this isn't to say that you should be looking over each team member's shoulder or following up behind them to the point of annoyance—or worst, the insinuation of mistrust. Remember, let your team be your team and get out of the way.

At the same time, never forget that they are your team because they have agreed to do things the *best* way—and you should have a thorough understanding of what that way is: how it looks when things are succeeding, and how it looks when things are failing. It is your responsibility to keep things in check.

Inspection is not only about taking responsibility for the final product, but also about being hands-on in the process that brings it into fruition. Jesus trained the disciples very well. Many times He would let them perform tremendous tasks on their own. Still, saving humanity was ultimately *His* mission. He never neglected to correct the disciples when they steered off course, and often enough He chose to perform particular works on his own to ensure they were done right.

At the end of the day, inspection is probably the single most important thing that you can do to *maintain* your success. It is the process of ensuring that all other processes are running smoothly and up to standard. It may take a bit of drudge work and, certainly, a critical eye. But you'll surely be glad to have caught a small fox before he's had a chance to spoil the vine in your Promised Land. Inspection is the key to maintaining victory.

***

So, there you have it: *3 Keys to Maintaining Victory*. As long as you know how to win and continue in the patterns of success, you'll never be a failure. Remain integral and approach each challenge with the spirit of innovation, inspecting the internal workings of your progress at each step of the way. Certainly, you'll be glad that you did. It is my prayer that you continue to win in life.

Chapter 11:
Share Your Story

On a final note: after you win the race, and as you continue winning in life, always be mindful of the fact that winning is never a solo act. Each winning experience is best enjoyed when it is shared with others. Whether they're cheering you on at the finish line or just hanging out in the stands in amazement—or even your competitors—there are people all around you that need to hear and share in your story.

Can you see what God has done for us through the gift of His living Word in the Bible, and by the example of His son Jesus Christ? God has given us the very instructions needed to win in our own lives and to be a part of His story, that He might be glorified in the things that He has called us to do and the goals that we desire to accomplish with His blessing.

Throughout this book, we have repeatedly referred to various Old and New Testament Scriptures, encouraged by the stories of the people of God:

From the story of Joseph, we learned to persevere in the midst of great persecution and that many times our enemies are the very people that are intended to push us into greatness. We came to an understanding that the prisons of life are sometimes the very incubators for the gifts and talents that will propel us to the palace.

From the story of Moses and the children of Israel, we learned that God is well-able to deliver us from our greatest adversaries and to usher us to the gates of the Promised Land, giving us strategies to conquer each step of the way. We learned that when faced with the fear of giants standing in the way of our inheritance, nothing can prevail against our God, His promises, and the great power that He has invested in us!

From the story of Abraham, we learned how it is often necessary to step out of our comfort zones in order to walk into the destiny that God has called and prepared us for. No, it isn't typically the easiest or most convenient thing to do. However, by faith, it is always the wisest and most rewarding decision.

From the story of Jesus Christ, we recognized His matchless wisdom in forming His team of disciples, and the components necessary to form a successful team able to handle a broad spectrum of situations: from Peter the right-hand man to Andrew the go-getter; from James and John the "Sons of thunder" to *Judas*, of which we should always beware.

From the story of Joshua, we learned the value of following God's instructions when going into battle. Your battle can be anything in life that's coming against you, or maybe just something that you have to conquer. Whatever it is, always be mindful that God knows what is best for you, and that He only has the best intentions toward you when it comes to seeing you to your Promised Land—even if this means Him instructing you to rest in Him for a while. Or who knows, before the battle is over, God may even tell you to save a Rahab.

Surely, we have learned from many stories throughout the Bible, and enclosing this book I'd like to share one last story with you. It is the story of an extraordinary woman by the name of Ruth. From it, we can gain great insight into the value of sharing one's journey toward success with others.

The story of Ruth goes as follows...

In the land of Bethlehem there lived a man named Elimelech. He lived with his wife, Naomi, and their two sons, Mahlon and Chilion. Unfortunately, there was a great famine in the land. And so, Elimelech sold his land, and moved his family to Moab hoping to find prosperity there. Unfortunately, soon after they arrived, Elimelech died. Nevertheless, the rest of the family continued in Moab, and each son married a Moabite woman: one named Orpah, and the other, Ruth.

For ten years, everything seemed to be fine. However, as it turned out, Mahlon and Chilion died, leaving two widows behind, and no children. The women were left alone to fend for themselves, and it seemed that the lineage of Elimelech would be lost forever. These grave times had convinced Naomi that the Lord was against her, and she decided to head back to Bethlehem. Her daughters-in-law were determined to go with her. But Naomi advised the women to stay behind in Moab and find husbands.

Orpah stayed behind. But Ruth remained faithful to Naomi, saying "...wherever you go, I will go; and wherever you lodge, I will lodge; your people shall be my people, and your God, my God..." (Ruth 1:16) Naomi was pleased and prayed the Lord's blessing upon Ruth. Together, the two went on to Bethlehem, and upon her return, the people recognized her and word of Naomi's condition spread throughout the land.

Meanwhile, Ruth came up with an idea as to how they could find food. It was the season of harvest, and Ruth decided to go and glean whatever was left over in the harvesting fields. It so happened that she came upon the field of a wealthy man named Boaz. He noticed her, and asked about her. He was told of her story with Naomi, and had compassion. Boaz gave Ruth permission to glean from his fields. He even invited her to dinner, and instructed his harvesters to respect her and intentionally leave food behind for her throughout the harvest season.

Ruth went back excited. She told Naomi about everything that had happened—about the generous rich man, Boaz. Naomi recognized the name, and told Ruth that Boaz was her late husband's relative.

Then, Naomi came up with an idea…

In the Hebrew customs of that day, when a woman's husband died, it was up to her husband's brother to marry her and keep the deceased husband's lineage going by having a son with her. If there was no brother, such responsibility fell on the next of kin. So, on the last day of the harvest, Naomi instructed Ruth to go to the harvest festivities that night, and share her story with Boaz—how that she was of the house of Elimelech, which had no sons. Naomi told Ruth that Boaz would know what to do.

Ruth did as she was told.

Boaz was impressed that Ruth had taken a liking to the idea of marrying him over younger men in the land who were also rich. Moreover, he had come to know her as a virtuous woman. Therefore, he made an announcement before the people: that he would restore the lineage of Elimelech by buying back the land Elimelech had sold and with it the right to Ruth's hand in marriage.

Boaz, who was Rahab's son, married Ruth.

And so, the house of Elimelech and Naomi were blessed; Ruth was blessed—and everyone else, for that matter. Boaz and Ruth had a son named Obed, who became the great grandfather of King David, a great patriarch in the lineage of our Lord and Savior, Jesus Christ.

***

There are many things that we can learn from the story of Ruth, the Moabite.

Ruth was definitely one to step out of her comfort zone. Though she was not of the children of Israel, something about the ways of the Hebrews attracted her, and she decided to follow Naomi and the God of Abraham, Isaac, and Jacob. Ruth's decision also probably had a lot to do with—if not more to do with—her relationship with Naomi. They had known each other for ten years as daughter-in-law and mother-in-law, and had apparently formed an inseparable bond—one that would not even be broken by the prospect of finding a husband and bearing children.

Have you ever known people who sacrificed their dreams to see that others were cared for? Perhaps, this is you: the mother who dropped out of college to take care of her newborn baby; the great athlete who could have gone on to the pros, but decided to train and mentor others instead; the doctor who may never find a cure for his own disease, but has nevertheless become a ready help for so many others.

It is true that most of the time we do not know where life will take us. Moreover, every so often we are faced with tough decisions that will significantly effect the direction in which we take our lives. The decision to invest in someone else and to share in their story should never be taken lightly, especially if the decision is likely to change the course of the investor's life.

Ruth had no guarantee that she would ever find a husband if she went to Bethlehem with Naomi. Yet, she went and continued to work faithfully toward Naomi's care—to find food. And this sacrifice of support was particularly meaningful, because at the time Naomi incorrectly believed that the Lord was against her. Though, her feelings were understandable: not only had her husband died, but her sons had also died, leaving no heirs behind.

God has very interesting ways of placing us on the right path to destiny. The Bible tells us that His ways are passed finding out. (Romans 11:33) His thinking is so far above ours, which is why it is important to trust Him. Many times God has placed you in the life of others to encourage them, and to let them know that He has not forgotten them. In turn, for your faithful service, God is just to reward you: sharing in someone else's story to see that their dreams are fulfilled will ultimately result in them sharing in your story and your dreams being fulfilled.

Had it not been for Ruth sharing in Naomi's story, she would have never crossed paths with Boaz, the wealthy man of God that she eventually married. Boaz personifies the Promised Land. He is a great testament to the truth that people reap what they sow. Ruth cared for Naomi and, in turn, Boaz cared for Ruth. Look at God!

And even though Ruth is the main character, the story can also be seen from the perspective of Boaz. Not only did Boaz do what he did for Ruth, but he also did it for the house of Elimelech. Though the Scriptures do not tell us how they were related, we know that Boaz felt it was important to remember his near kin. Boaz decided to share his story and allow the lineage of Elimelech to prosper through him.

Sharing your story is about looking beyond yourself and seeing the big picture. Just as Joshua saved Rahab, who would give birth to Boaz, Boaz saved Ruth, who would give birth to—if you go all the way down the line—Jesus Christ! Ruth never imagined that the Savior of the world would be a direct descendant of her family tree. But He was! And you never know how far your contribution to the greater good will go. Therefore, it is important to not simply hold on to the wealth of your success, in whatever form it may be. Share it! The victory is not just yours, but it belongs to the entire kingdom of God.

Now, granted, you may not think your story is all that grand or glorious. But this shouldn't stop you from sharing it. When Naomi returned to Bethlehem, she was terribly devastated, having lost her husband and two sons, with no grandchildren. It would have been easy enough for her to hide away from the people that recognized her. However, she decided to share her story with them and eventually word got to Boaz, who decided to have compassion on Ruth because of what he had *heard*. Has anyone heard your story yet?

You may be tempted to think that you're the only one going through what you're going through, or that you're all by yourself and no one cares. Yes, you may feel this way even now. But it is important for you to know—and God wants you to know—someone cares for you! The trials of your journey have not been in vain. Something great can still come from your testimony so long as you are willing to share it.

Don't be afraid of what people are going to think and say. The road to victory takes us through many changes, and there are different types of success. Some successes can only be found in the darkest hour just before day—and, of necessity, many times you must arrive to your darkest hour before you can behold the light of a new day. Don't be ashamed to share the story of God's amazing grace in your situation. Somebody wants to hear it. And don't let anything cause you to give up on winning in life. God has an awesome plan with you in mind!

The essence of Ruth's story rests in the understanding that we should follow God. Ruth said that she would follow Naomi *and* her God. As long as you follow God, your story is guaranteed to have a happy ending. It may take patience and hard work to see it through: you may have to sacrifice some of your desires to help a Naomi; you may have to glean in a new field, learning to work in an area far beyond your comfort zone; you may have to place yourself at the feet of a Boaz, positioning yourself to receive the promise of a great inheritance.

Now, as you can see, I told the story of Ruth and Boaz—moving straight to the happy ending. However, there was a plot twist that I chose to reserve for this moment to bring home a very important point:

When Ruth first told Boaz her story, that she was the daughter-in-law of the deceased Elimelech, Boaz knew where she was going—even though she didn't come right out and say it. Gladly, seeing that she was a virtuous woman, in that moment, he basically expressed his desire to marry her after the Hebrew customs in order to restore the lineage of Elimelech. But the plot thickened when he told her that he *wasn't* her nearest of kin. There was another man in Bethlehem who was more closely related to Ruth than Boaz. And, according to the Hebrew custom, Boaz had to check with him first to see if he wanted to marry Ruth instead.

So even if Boaz says yes, things still may not go as smoothly as you hope. Ruth and Boaz had met: a victory in and of itself. Nonetheless, there was something standing in the way of their marriage.

Have you ever achieved a certain level of victory, but something was standing in the way of you "marrying" your full destiny? It could have been a small thing or something relatively large: qualified for the promotion, but not having the necessary scholastic degree; almost to the point of finding a breakthrough solution, but running out of funding; knowing that you have the potential to do awesome things, but unable to get over depression and low self-esteem because of the events of your past.

Yes, there are things that can hold us back. However, if we are to conquer them, we must face them head on and share our story. Boaz went straight to the other relative and told him what was going on. And, as it was the will of God, things worked to Boaz's favor.

Remember that God is faithful and that He will never allow your destiny to be withheld from you on account of an irrelevant technicality. God has no interest in nitpicking through the requirements for success because the only real requirement is that you be in Him, for He is the author and finisher of our faith. (Hebrews 12:2) When the time comes to boldly meet the final level of your ultimate victory, be comforted that God has brought you to the place of your Promised Land, and that His promises are forever "Yes and Amen!"

So, Boaz married Ruth. He made a grand announcement before all the people that they might share in the beauty of the story as well. People need to see restoration—they need a *visual*. There's someone out there that needs to know that dreams do come true. You may be the very one whose story will propel them into the fulfillment of their dreams.

In Jewish culture there's a great tradition of storytelling. Through the Bible, God continually instructed His people to remember their history and to share their story, generation after generation, about the various people and events responsible for Israel arriving to place that God desired for it. He instructed them to not only share the victories, but also the failures, and all the determining steps in between.

Every aspect of your journey counts because each facet of your life affects the outcome—not only in your life, but also the lives of others. Sharing your story is about perpetuating the mentality of a champion, telling others what it takes to win, what it takes to endure, what it takes to look beyond the circumstances of life—beyond the "no win" situations, and the fears that most of us have to face at some point in our lives.

Winning in life is a team effort. You will not win alone. At the same time, you must realize that you're *never* alone! God is with you always; and, He has put people on your path to help you win. It is simply up to you to embrace the process of victory, to run your race looking ahead, with your head held high and your eyes on the finish line.

Now go out, and win! The victory is yours!

Chapter 12:
The Greatest Investment

The greatest investment that you will ever make will not be with you investing in your earthly future but in your eternal future. God is a God of wealth, health, and happiness but throughout the Scriptures He places emphasis on spiritual riches. Jesus said, "For where your treasure is, there will your heart be also." (Matthew 6:21) No one would dare put all of their money in a bank vault and then forget the name of the bank or its location. Yet, many bank on living on this earth without Jesus Christ as their personal Savior. They seem to forget that their name is not written in the Lamb's book of life, and they forget where they will not spend eternity if they don't make "a wise investment."

Colossians 3:2 says, "Set your affection on things above not on things on the earth." Be grateful for all of your blessings, but don't allow your earthly gain to supersede your heavenly treasure. The Bible tells us, "We have this treasure in earthen vessels." (II Corinthians 4:7) The Holy Spirit is deposited in the life of every born-again believer and we have the right and privilege to make a spiritual withdrawal from this heavenly account throughout our Christian lives. If you've made the wisest investment of a lifetime, you too have a right to the spiritual riches of God's anointing and power.

Some will say, "I don't need God's spiritual riches. I've got my own riches." But Jesus said, "What shall it profit a man, if he shall gain the *whole* world, and lose his own soul? (Mark 8:36) He said, "A man's life consists not in the abundance of the things which he possesses."

Then Jesus spoke a parable to his disciples saying, "The ground of a certain rich man brought forth plentifully: And he thought within himself, saying, 'What shall I do, because I have no room where to bestow my fruits?' And he said, 'This will I do: I will pull down my barns, and build greater; and there will I bestow all my fruits and my goods. And I will say to my soul, Soul thou hast much goods laid up for many years; take thine ease, eat, drink, and be merry. But God said unto him, Thou fool, this night thy soul shall be required of thee: then whose shall those things be, which thou hast provided? So is he that lays up treasure for himself, and is not rich toward God." (Luke 12:15-21)

The Scriptures let us know that this rich man had planned to continue living, with plenty, for many years. And he wasn't planning on anything going wrong. Have you made plans for the next fifteen, twenty, or thirty years? Have you also planned a "merry" life without Jesus? What if now is your last opportunity to make this wise investment?

Some will say, "I'm not like the rich man. I plan to turn my whole life over to God. But there are things I need, right now. Things I want to accomplish in this world."

Do you know what the Bible says about *things*? "Seek ye *first* the kingdom of God, and his righteous; and all these things shall be added unto you." Now, some things may be added to your life one at a time and other things may be multiplied ten times over. But things will be added when you put first things first. And you can't beat God adding no matter how hard you try.

You may say, "But will this make me rich?" The Bible says, "The blessing of the Lord, it makes rich, and he adds no sorrow with it." (Proverbs 10:22) The Hebrew translation for the word blessing in this verse of scripture is *berakah* (*ber-aw-kaw*) meaning *prosperity*.

Not only does the prosperity of God put you in a successful, flourishing, and thriving condition. He causes your *circumstances* to be prosperous. Now that's rich! How many people have you known who had wealth, but not even their money and resources could fix their circumstances. Many times circumstances take authority over money, stuff, and things. But the *blessing* of the Lord takes authority over circumstances with no sorrow added with it. And "no good thing will he withhold from them that walk uprightly." (Psalm 84:11)

Are you walking upright? Are you living a life of faith?

In case you didn't know, that's what the victorious Christian life is all about—walking up right and living a life of faith! The golden key to winning in life is salvation, and without it you're lost. After all, whoever heard of a lost winner? Winners are goal-oriented. They finish what they start. They know their way to the finish line. They accept the challenges and spit in the face of mediocrity.

It's a challenge to resist the temptations of this world and say, "For God I live and for God I'll die," but it's what those who *truly* are winning in life do. I challenge you to come aboard and begin totally winning in life today.

Some may say, "I don't have any really big sins in my life. So, I don't need to go overboard with this Christian thing." Well, I think it's safe to say when one Man died on the cross, for the sins of the whole world that was going way overboard. But that's what Jesus did! The Bible says, "For when we were yet helpless and without strength, at the right time, Christ died for the ungodly. For scarcely for a righteous man will one die: yet possibly for a good man some would even dare to die. But God showed his love toward us, in that, while we were yet sinners, Christ died for us." (Romans 5:6-8) That's awesome!

Perhaps your question, at this point is, "What must I do to receive salvation and begin winning in life today?"

The Bible says, "Repent, and be baptized every one of you in the name of Jesus Christ for the forgiveness of your sins; and you shall receive the gift of the Holy Spirit." (Acts 2:38) By simply confessing with your mouth that Jesus is Lord and believing in your heart that God raised him from the dead salvation is made available to you. (Romans 10:9)

Will you begin "Winning in Life" today?